CW00536678

I Wish I Knew

I Wish
I Knew

Honest and real lessons on love,
life and family as you grow

GEORGIA KOUSOULOU

SEVEN DIALS

First published in Great Britain in 2024 by Seven Dials,
an imprint of The Orion Publishing Group Ltd
Carmelite House, 50 Victoria Embankment
London EC4Y 0DZ

An Hachette UK Company

1 3 5 7 9 10 8 6 4 2

A CIP catalogue record for this book is
available from the British Library.

ISBN (Hardback) 978 1 3996 1983 7
ISBN (eBook) 978 1 3996 1984 4
ISBN (Audio) 978 1 3996 1985 1

Typeset by Bryony Clark
Printed in Great Britain by Clays Ltd, Elcograf S.p.A.

MIX
Paper from
responsible sources
FSC® C104740
FSC
www.fsc.org

www.orionbooks.co.uk

To Brody, the love of my life.

Thank you for making me your mummy x

CONTENTS

INTRODUCTION

Me or Mum?

Hello, I'm Georgia.

You might know me from *The Only Way Is Essex* (otherwise known as TOWIE), my show *Baby Steps*, or my podcast *Five Minutes Peace*. I now know me as 'Brody's mum'. That's how I tell people who I am, and what I do: I look after my two-year-old son Brody.

When I became a mum, I lost my own identity a bit. I always talk about Brody first now; as a parent, my life revolves around him, of course. He's the first thing I think about when I wake up, the last thing I think of as I fall asleep. When you become a mum, it's almost expected that that is entirely what you become – Mum with a capital 'M'.

So, I wanted to write this book, for all of us – for anyone who has ever felt not enough, or who needed to hear someone else saying what they were thinking.

And I always say what I think! So, welcome!

This is the book I needed growing up, too. It's the book I wish I'd had when I was younger, when I didn't know what was in my future. I hope it shows the down-to-earth perspective I've always had, and that reading this feels like talking to your best mate. When I first became a mum, I'd have loved a book that just made me feel *normal*. You're expected to know a lot, aren't you? And you don't always want to ask people every little thing that pops into your head. I used to get embarrassed asking questions – literally, anything! – because I thought people would think I was stupid, or not good enough. But those questions aren't silly and I'm going to answer as many of them as I can here. So, if you're looking for a bit of advice and to feel like you're having a chat with your friend, read on!

It's everything I wish I had known, and so much more . . .

Love,

Georgia x

I wish I knew ...

I love being pregnant

When I was younger, I always wanted children. I'd be the one looking after my younger siblings or playing with all my cousins. I was the eldest and I was always in charge. I liked looking after all of them. I still do.

When Mum and Dad separated when I was in my twenties, though, it threw me. I didn't know what I wanted from life after that. I went through a really weird process of almost unravelling. My family life as I knew it was gone, so I didn't have an idea of what a family was any more. It had to change, and that in turn changed me. The thought of planning to have a child, back then, freaked me out! Now I can look back and laugh at younger me, because planning a baby is all well and good, but it doesn't really happen that way. You can't plan a baby into being. You can do everything to help it happen, of course. Brody happened by accident, and I don't know how it happened so quickly . . .

I was on the pill from the age of fifteen. I didn't have a boyfriend (other people were on the pill to have sex but I wasn't!).

Around the age of twenty-eight, I thought, *Maybe I'll have a baby when I'm thirty, or at least start thinking about it then.* On my twenty-ninth birthday, I had my birthday party, and then I came off the pill. All of a sudden, it was making me feel sick. I'd been on it for fourteen years with only one year's break, as I used to get really bad period pains. I've only just found out now that it's because I've got polycystic ovaries. It had got to the point where I'd take the pill every day but the thought of it made me gag. I thought it was my body telling me to come off it.

Everyone said that was a good idea, because if

you want a baby, the pill takes a year and a half to come out of your system anyway.

Well, that's a lie. I wish I'd known that it didn't take a year and a half, because I had one period, had sex once and got pregnant. I literally had sex once. It took me a while to realise I was pregnant, though. I started feeling *really* weird. I remember drinking a cup of tea (I'm obsessed with tea – a cup of PG Tips – I'm addicted) and I couldn't get through it. I was getting very odd feelings because everything tasted weird. My friend Maddie said, 'Do a pregnancy test,' and I said, 'Don't be so stupid.' I did a test, and it was negative. I told her I wasn't pregnant. She said, 'No, you are. Do another in a week's time.'

I didn't really believe her but I did it all the same. That's what friends are for, right? Telling you to do things that are good for you? That second time, it said very clearly: pregnant. I was so shocked, I thought it had to be wrong; it was definitely wrong. I couldn't believe it. I ran into the bedroom, and said to my fiancé, 'Tom, I'm pregnant!' He was in bed, asleep, and said, 'Whaaaat?' I remember adding, though, 'I don't know if I am.' I was so confused!

Tom told me to do another test, so I rang my friend Beau, who does my make-up, and said I needed a favour. She said, 'You want me to get you a pregnancy test.' I had no idea how she knew. She said she'd be round in a minute, as she was coming to do my make-up anyway to film TOWIE that day.

Beau and Tommy were waiting outside the bathroom while I was doing the test, and once the result was clear, I gasped, 'I'm pregnant.' It was the biggest shock of my life. I'm still shocked now, and I've got a child . . .

I was excited but also so scared, because I'd never changed a nappy, never fed a baby. I knew I wanted kids some day, but this day had turned into some day! I did feel maternal, but not overly so. Before having a baby, I might see a baby and think, *Oh, cute*, but I'd see a dog and be like, *OH MY GOD, CUTE*. Even when my friends had babies, I wasn't a natural 'pick up and help with the baby' type. It wouldn't come naturally to me. So, I panicked. My best friend had a baby at this point, and I really loved them, but I got to give the baby back. I wouldn't with my own, so I freaked out a lot.

Childbirth had also always scared me. When I was younger, I'd say to my mum, 'I don't think I'll ever be able to do this. How did you do it?' I used to ask her loads of questions about it. I didn't like the idea of planning a baby either, the commitment scared me! For me, it was better that it just happened in the way it did, because I'm a control freak too. I needed the idea that it was a decision that was out of my hands! That sounds so funny now, but it's the truth!

The further into my pregnancy I got, the more excited I became. I just knew I had to learn fast. Everyone said you learn on the job, so I went with it. I felt completely normal throughout my pregnancy, except for a travel sickness feeling until I was about thirteen weeks. I felt really tired all the time, and that was the worst thing about it. It probably didn't help that I was filming TOWIE a lot. That meant really early starts and late nights, and I couldn't tell anyone. I remember turning up to *TOWIE* late and the cameramen would ask if I was OK and I'd be like, 'Yeah, why?' And they'd say, 'You're never late, what's going on?' I had to tell the exec producer, Luke, who I love and is still a good friend of mine. I told him the day I found out I was pregnant because I knew he knew me, and I needed him to be on board. We started *TOWIE* at the same time so we had a special bond. It was actually Luke and Cheryl's (a *TOWIE* exec as well as the time) idea to have my and Tommy's baby show!

I loved when we got to announce it on *TOWIE*. I didn't tell any of the cast that I was pregnant, and I still don't know how I kept it a secret for that long. I didn't tell anyone – not even my mum and dad – until I was ten weeks. I was so paranoid, and I just couldn't believe it, so I had loads of scans and didn't tell anyone until I saw a proper heartbeat on the baby.

I decided to save the *TOWIE* announcement until the Christmas special. I wanted everyone's real-life reactions. Chloe Sims, who I was really close to at the time, couldn't understand how I'd kept it a secret. They'd started thinking things because I kept turning down nights out (and I loved a night out!). I knew they were on to me so I started saying things like, 'I really want a pornstar martini tonight,' to throw them off.

What I actually desperately wanted was a Coke Zero! It became my main craving, so much so that now I can't drink it because I drank so much of it then! I loved McDonald's too, but then again I always love McDonald's. I wanted it all the time and I craved carbs. That still hasn't gone away either! I couldn't drink tea until I was about fourteen or fifteen weeks pregnant, it was just Coke! But don't worry, I started easing myself back into a cup once a day, twice a day max (instead of my usual five). I was genuinely really scared I was going to go off tea for life!

I only found out after giving birth that my placenta was at the front, covering my belly, so I didn't feel any kicks. Getting bigger and growing a baby but not feeling the movements meant it never felt real until Brody was actually in my arms.

I loved that I was growing a child, though. I was so happy during that period of my life, so content. Everyone treats you so nicely when you're pregnant, and it made me super laidback. I was on *TOWIE* all the way through but I was so calm. Someone told me that your baby will be how you were when you were pregnant, and it really stuck with me, so I was mindful of how I was feeling. I tried to be as chilled and relaxed as possible and so I swear that person was right, because Brody is so chilled.

I was so happy, and I thought pregnancy was the best thing ever, and I'm sure what added to that feeling was being really confident in my body. It was interesting to me, to not feel self-conscious, as obviously I've never had a belly like I had then. But I really wanted to show off my belly in tight dresses. I think that comes down to the fact that since the age of twenty-two, I've been on telly, and so there's always been a certain type of pressure to be in the gym.

This was the first time I could relax in my body, and it was such an empowering feeling. So my advice to you is, get your belly out! Celebrate your bump, celebrate your ability to carry a child. Before, if I wanted to wear a tight dress, I'd have gone on a diet and panicked about it constantly, but being pregnant, I didn't care at all. I could wear a tight dress, eat McDonald's, and it was the best thing ever.

I did get sciatica when I was pregnant, which was really painful. But other than that, my experience was very positive. Obviously it was hard, as you change in every way, but then I reasoned that I was growing a child, so it was bound to happen to me. I didn't feel a connection with my bump, I wasn't thinking, *I've got a little boy growing in there.* I don't think I actually connected to him until he was here. Now I know it was normal but, at the time, I wasn't sure if there was something wrong with the way I was feeling.

I thought the pregnancy was going to feel like it lasted a long time, and I genuinely would have been happy if it had lasted two years! I really did love it that much.

Brody turned breech in the January; everyone

said he would move but I knew deep down he wouldn't. I guess I always knew I was never pushing him out because looking back at all the online hypnobirthing classes I was way too calm . . . and for someone who had always been scared of giving birth, that was weird!

Did I manifest this? Or was this my first taste of mother's intuition?

After giving birth, though, it was hard. I describe my birth like going shopping. With a C-section, you have the date, you know where you're going and when. It was in my diary marked as 'baby coming'. You enter hospital pregnant, then come out and you're not. Someone gives you this human, this baby, that they say is yours, and I remember thinking, *If I didn't see them cut me open, I'd have thought the baby could have come from anywhere.*

Having a C-section meant that I didn't physically push Brody out, and I do really believe my body didn't know I'd had the baby it had been looking after for so long. It took a while for the reality of having a baby to settle in. I went into complete shock mode – mentally and physically. All I was thinking was, *What the fuck is this life? What am I doing? How can I go from feeling so happy, living my best life, to this? Now what?*

Five minutes' peace when you're pregnant:

- *Sit with a cup of tea and listen to a podcast. It's an amazing way of finding connection or just a bit of entertainment, and there are so many different types to choose from.*

- *Sit in the nursery where your baby will sleep and feel the energy around you in that room. Close your eyes, breathe in, and remember you're going to be OK.*

- *Enjoy the calm (before the chaos!).*

♡

'I knew I wanted kids
some day, but **this** day
had turned into
some day!'

♡

I wish I knew ...

It's OK to take a long time to find your passion in life

♡

I always used to say to my mum when I was growing up, 'I want to be a TV presenter.' I remember her saying, 'Georgia, if you don't get your grades, you won't get there.' When I was in school, people would ask me, 'What's your passion?' I didn't know what to say because I'd never actually done TV, so I had no idea if I was good at it (or even if I would like it at all). I was never good at sports, never academic. The only thing I was good at was being social with my friends! Looking back now, I wish I'd known that people were my thing, my passion – and that that is enough to get you where you want to be. But

15

I struggled with not having the same kind of skills my friends all seemed to have. My friends were good at beauty or hairdressing or sport. Everyone appeared to know what their thing was. That meant they all seemed to know for sure what they wanted to do, but more importantly, how to get there.

I'd say I wanted to be a presenter as a child, but as I got into my teen years, I'd never say it out loud because I'd be too embarrassed. I thought, *I'm never going to do TV, it's too far away from my real life.*

I struggled with what I *was* good at. I tried Irish dancing, kickboxing, cheerleading, other types of dance. I tried everything and I was never good at any of it!

I remember one teacher saying, 'You're lucky you're pretty.' I think he meant it in a nice way, but I remember thinking, *I'm not even that pretty. And also, how will being pretty help me anyway?!*

I really struggled with maths at school. English was my best subject, but I had a tutor for both subjects my whole life thanks to my parents. I tell my mum this now, but it actually damaged me, having a tutor. Although it was good for me, and I get why they did that – and I'll do it for Brody too, if he needs extra help – but it damaged me mentally because it always made me feel I was never good enough on my own. It always made me feel I was behind, which I was, but I lost confidence in myself. Bless my mum – I had to have a tutor, as the only GCSE I passed was English. But it did have another effect of making me think I wasn't clever at all.

Looking back now, my mum was doing the best she could to try to help me, and I was lucky we were able to afford it. But I didn't know that back then; I just thought I had a tutor because I was the dumb one. In reality, I just needed a bit of extra help, and it wasn't a bad thing, but because we all compare ourselves to our friends at that age (and even now), and my friends weren't doing it, it meant it wasn't good.

I don't know where I got the idea that I wanted to be a presenter all those years ago. As I got older, I'd watch Holly Willoughby and absolutely love her skills at interviewing and creating a show that was fun to watch, but I don't know where I first got the idea. When no one acknowledges that you're good at something, you don't know what's in the future. I knew I had a lot of friends, and got on with everyone, but no one took notice of that as a strength. It would have been so different if someone had said to me that I could work in TV or do something in a similar industry because I was really talkative and chatty. But no one picked that up. Back then, it wasn't something that felt possible, or attainable. My parents just wanted me to be happy. They knew I wasn't academic and they didn't push me to do academic stuff. They wanted me to study and pay attention at school and, with the tutor's help, I managed to pass GCSE English. They never mentioned university to me, whereas with my sister, Grace, they did. She was definitely going to uni.

I think I may have manifested my career. Before you roll your eyes – or perhaps you are eagerly nodding – I really believe in manifestation. I also believe your stars align when they are meant to. You can change your path, if you really want to, and if you're meant to do something, you'll do it.

In between wanting to be a presenter and getting on TV, I got into fashion. I loved clothes and dressing up nicely, and still do. My mum and dad had clothes shops, so I thought maybe that's something I'd like to do too. Maybe that's the thing I would be good at? By this point, I'd left school and tried college briefly, studying fashion, but I got chucked out. They'd sold it as a styling course, but it wasn't – it was really technical. I wasn't technical, so I struggled with that side of it. And then I gave up. I don't have a lot of self-belief. I remember I had to make a dress and I got my Greek nan, my *yaya*, to make it for me – she had factories when she was younger so knew exactly what she was doing. She did it for me and she made a seventies-style yellow dress with daisies on it. It was really short, so cute – and I passed, but it didn't make a difference because I didn't continue after the first year.

I left school when I was fifteen, and how are you supposed to know what you're meant to do at that age? Now you have to stay in education until you're eighteen, but even then, you're still so young. How can you make any big choice about what to do when you haven't experienced anything yet? I actually think a lot of people don't know what they want to do for a really long time throughout their lives. Some people just have more confidence than others, and so take bigger risks. I always say you're a very lucky person if you know what you want to do; you're blessed. Because otherwise, you've got to keep going round the houses and trying things until you know.

I love my work and wouldn't change it for the world but if I *had* to do something else, the only other job I've ever considered doing is being a private investigator. I love finding things out . . . Being a private investigator would really suit me, I think, but to do that back when I was younger, I would have needed the grades and to go to uni. I'm so lucky, though, because I'm doing something I love now.

I did an internship at *Fabulous* magazine for three months after college. I made myself indispensable and they offered me a fashion assistant job. I did that for a while but left because I wasn't ready for a full-time job at eighteen. I still had no confidence – working in magazine publishing, you've got to be really assertive. I wasn't!

It was also the first time I noticed that not having a degree hadn't stopped me. That's when I first started getting a little bit of self-belief. Working in the magazine industry seemed really serious at that age. It was quite overwhelming, and I was thinking, *Is this what I really want to do?*

That's when I started realising I'd got a job as a result of simply being me. Chatting to people, being friendly, just being myself. That was a quality that I hadn't seen as useful in a job setting before.

After I left the job, I knew I needed money. Mum and Dad weren't going to just fund my life! But I was still feeling quite empty and clueless – where were my passions? Why was I making such serious decisions at such a young age? Why are we all forced to?

I went to a job interview to be an office assistant

and the office was full of all these young women. I loved it. Waiting for the interview, I spent about twenty minutes chatting to all the girls who worked there. When it came to the interview, the interviewer sang my praises but stopped and said, 'But I'm not going to give you the job.' I was so upset. He said, 'If I give you this job, it'll be like caging a bird. You're not supposed to be working in this office. You'll be bored. And you'll leave straight away.'

At the time, I was devastated. Now, I think, *Who was this man who spent twenty minutes with me and came out thinking so much of me?* He was right. He saw something in me and turning me down for the role was the best thing he could have done. I always wondered why my school didn't pick up on things like that, encourage so many other different career routes? They see you for years and don't pick up on your real potential.

I knew I was in a lucky position because both of my parents owned their own businesses. I knew fashion, got on with people, and so my mum and dad started helping me look for a shop to call my own. We looked at a few but they kept falling through, and then one in Epping came up and that was the one. It was in the middle of the high street, such a good spot. It was also on the corner of an alleyway where there were nightclubs. I hoped the girls going to the clubs would see it and pop in to buy something (and that's exactly what happened). One of the best things, though, was that it had rooms I could rent out upstairs to help pay half the total rent. It was a massive risk because it was a ten-year lease with no break clause and my mum went mad, saying it was too risky. But Dad said, 'No, this opportunity is way too good to turn down.' He really believed in the shop. And, I suppose, in me.

At this time, TOWIE had already started on TV and me and my friends would see people from our area in it and think, *What the fuck is that?* A lot of people I went to school with were on TOWIE. I did get approached a couple of times when I was out and about with my friends, and they'd say, 'Would you mind being in the back of this shot?' And we'd be like, 'Yeah, fuck it, lovely!' like the extras on shows. The producers then had my number and would ring me, saying they needed me to be in the background again and I'd be like, 'Why not.'

One day, I was in the shop and this man came in and said, 'My daughter does teeth-whitening, she's amazing, I need to rent a room off you.' They were already rented out but he kept coming back. The third time he came in, he brought in his daughter Grace and I got on with her straight away. I said that my hairdresser, Jess, came in part-time so Grace could come in the rest of the time, and rent the same room. I'd have two people renting then and make more money from the room. I'd worked out a plan to be as financially responsible as I could.

Grace and I clicked straight away. She'd come in the shop even when she wasn't working. And then one day, she came in and said, 'I've been approached to go on TOWIE.' She said, 'The only problem with TOWIE is they need a friend to come on with me. I can't go on my own, they want two girls. So I've put your name forward.' I thought she was lying. Why didn't she put her other friends forward?

I remember getting a missed call on the Friday after, a voicemail from a woman called Anne. I called her back and we got on so well. She asked to come and see me the following Monday. By the next Monday, I was on TOWIE filming. It was so quick, I don't even think I signed anything! I didn't even have time to tell some of my family members. TOWIE wouldn't tell you if you were on the show or not each episode; they'd keep you guessing. They'd say, 'You're filming next week,' and we'd get on with it, but I never knew if I'd actually be featured. I just went with it. It was mad, but I loved it.

We were filming six days a week at one point, and it was so fun – I was young, truly living my best life! The shop was great but it was hard graft and I would need to work there six days too. I'd stop filming, go back to the shop. Mum would cover for me when I was filming, and I was very lucky to have her help. But the more I was on the show, the more they needed me as the more scenes I was doing. I realised very quickly I couldn't do both.

Before I went on TOWIE, I'd converted the shop from just a clothes shop into a one-stop-shop. I'd added in sunbeds, hair, make-up and beauty. You could come and get your clothes, have a sunbed, do your hair and make-up then go to the club next door! I went on TOWIE at exactly the wrong time. The shop needed full-time management because what I'd created required so many more people to keep it running. I thought I'd made a mistake trying to do both.

I needed to sell the shop before it went under. A girl who was working for me in-house, doing eyebrow tattooing, had heard I was selling it and bought it off me. I didn't even put it on the market. Bear in mind, I had a long lease – a ten-year lease – so if that woman hadn't paid the rent, obviously it would've gone to court but, ultimately, I would've been responsible for it. So it was a risk for about eight years. But they did really well. They saw the lease through then sold it as they had kids and couldn't run it any more.

It all worked out perfectly. The child Georgia

would be so happy to see me now. I do feel like we proved everyone wrong.

I always had the feeling that I wasn't good enough. Back in the day, people might have looked down on me for saying I wanted to do TV so to know that I've actually gone ahead and done it, I think that little girl would be feeling a bit smug, and thinking, *God, all I needed to do was believe in myself and know I was enough.* I think she would be really proud of me.

I've always trusted in the process. When I was on TOWIE, I thought I'd always be on it. But then when I had Brody, it didn't make sense to go back. I never thought about having my own show, though, it just happened. Everything seems to just unravel as it's meant to. My show keeps getting commissioned, and I'm so thankful for that, but of course that decision is based on viewing figures. I never know if it will get another series, which is wild. But things keep happening in life – not all good – that keep us going. We film life as it happens, and I'm just rolling with it.

I love contracts to feel stable and secure. Nothing beats a one-year contract to know we're going to be OK, and I'm lucky I now get to work with brands I really believe in on social media too. But always around New Year, I have a panic. I'll phone my manager and say, 'Oh my god, what am I doing with my life? What am I doing? I don't know what work's coming in.' And she'll say, 'Georgia, chill out. You do this every year. You've got things coming.' And then I remember I can believe in the process.

You can strive for what you want, and I do write down what I want for each year. But it's not my personality to dream big. Maybe I could be doing so much more if I was that way, but I'm not. I'm generally quite content with my life. I know there are other girls on the same agency books who will see someone else getting a job and they'll call and say, 'Why isn't that me?' I'm not that girl. As long as I've got a few jobs coming in, a bit of money, I'm happy. It's also easier to manifest from a place of contentment. Tommy's always striving for more, and most people want to earn more money and do more and more, but I'm happy plodding along. So you can't always have it all, and I think having to wait for things is sometimes exactly what you really need to know what matters.

'I believe your stars align when they are meant to. You can change your path, if you really want to'

Manifesting tips

If you'd like to try manifesting like I do, here are some tips:

- *Start when you are in a place of contentment and want to have a go.*

- *Get clear on your big, overarching dream (for me, that was to be on TV).*

- *Write three reasons you'd be good at doing that. Self-confidence is key.*

- *Trust the process and know that it will happen when it's meant to.*

- *In the meantime, keep busy and make sure you're working to earn the money you need.*

- *When you see angel numbers, always say thank you for what you want, like it's already yours, e.g. 'Thank you for my promotion at work.' I do this three times every time. Angel numbers are recurring numbers or numbers in a special sequence, like 11:11, 12:12, etc.*

- *Always write down that you're thankful that what you're manifesting is yours.*

- *You have to believe and act like you have what you're trying to manifest already.*

- *When the dream starts to come true, grab it with both hands.*

- *Work hard, but rest lots.*

- *Surround yourself with people you love and who support and boost you.*

- *Know that if you're meant to continue on that path, you will.*

- *Always be grateful for what you've already got.*

- *Enjoy life. It's about the small, everyday joys as well as the big wins.*

I wish I knew ...

The 2 a.m. night-feed silence is deafening

I love sleep. But, sorry, what is sleep? I haven't had unbroken sleep since before I was pregnant. I had insomnia when I was pregnant (how unlucky is that? Good practice, some people said. Very funny) and it's never gone away! I really struggled with the 2 a.m. wake-up calls because I so rarely got back to sleep. Looking back now, though, I realise it doesn't last. It's just a phase. It's just that when you're in it, it feels like it's going to last forever and it can feel like such a scary, lonely place.

I used to love a lie-in – didn't we all? I've always enjoyed a good night's sleep and never, not at one point, considered the impact a baby would have on it. What I also didn't realise was that a lack of sleep really affects your mood.

What I find crazy is how women are expected to have babies and no sleep, and then are expected to live a normal life. After I had Brody, I took my hat off to all the mums I'd ever known. I thought, *Wow, how have you all just been doing this without complaining?* Everyone around me had the mindset of just getting on with it. Society makes them, and it's sad, because support and understanding are the two most important things for a new mum, I think.

I found those night feeds so lonely. It's *so* quiet. It feels like no one else in the world is awake, and you're the only one who has to be up, being useful, being there. There were some sweet moments when it was nice, when I felt good about myself, but generally, I would dread nights. I'd go to bed knowing what was going to happen – that I would have to wake up. So, I started doing night-time selfies and sharing them on Instagram, saying, 'Mums, are you here? Where are the 2 a.m. mums?'

And when people would message me back, I'd feel better. It helped to know there were so many others going through the same thing. I wasn't alone any more.

What's especially hard is when you've had so little sleep that you feel tearful the next day because of it. I mean, I am a tearful person anyway, I'm always ready to cry! But adding the tiredness on top of the hormones really made me struggle, and I know it's the same for so many other parents.

Tommy and I decided to try something different. Tommy started doing the 5 a.m. feed and so I'd go back to bed until 9 a.m. and have a block of a few hours. That saved me. He'd take responsibility and I could just rest, knowing Brody was being looked after and everything was OK. I would settle when Brody was taken out of the room.

I said no to help with the night feeds in the early days; I guess I wanted to prove I was a good mum or something and didn't need the help. I wish I knew that it makes you no less of a mum for accepting help; in fact it makes you a brave, honest, good mum . . . we all need the help. My advice would be: always say yes to help. You are human! There were evenings when I'd cry because I was dreading the night feeds so much. And then my support system kicked in with my mum or Tommy's mum, Bev, coming in and helping out. The nans, as I call them, were amazing.

Tommy was working a lot at that time so it was really hard to feel like there was enough of me to go around. It wasn't the best time, but the nans would take Brody in his little crib and I'd wave goodbye, lock the door and have such a good night's sleep. Then after that, I'd be all right for a few days. Getting that relief every now and then really helped. It was like a reset.

It's one of the hardest parts of motherhood, the lack of sleep. But then when you're getting sleep, there's always something else that comes along that's just as hard. With newborns, I found the nights harder but the days easier, and in the toddler stage, the nights are easier but the days are harder. Yeah, we all sleep now but the days are *full-on*. Back when Brody was a newborn, I could sit and have a full dinner and watch *Loose Women*. Now, he'll get me up at 6.30 a.m., get all the toys out by 6.35 a.m. and by 8 a.m. you feel like you've done a full day.

After about three and a half months, Brody was in his own room. But in those first months, it felt like the sleepless nights were going to go on forever and I'd never get out of waking up. I described it like a black tunnel, where you can't see the light. I was a bit depressed, which might seem quite harsh for some people to hear, but that's how it was for me. Every day, I was doing the same mundane things. I'd dread the nights but I'd also come to dread the days. As soon as it got dark, I'd panic and be in constant fear. But it does get easier, it passes. Everything really is a phase. If I'd known that, I'd have been better. Second time round, I will be better.

The 2 a.m. Club

For you, here are some positive quotes to have a read through when you're up in the night and feeling a bit fed up . . .

You're not alone.

You're stronger than you think.

You are enough.

You're doing an **amazing** job.

You'll get through this soon.

Time moves quickly.

This is just a phase.

So soon, you'll have smashed another night.

Questions to remind yourself
how well you're doing:

1. *Name one thing you did well yesterday ...*
   (E.g. Got out for a walk with my baby)

_____

_____

_____

2. *What's the biggest win so far this week?*
   (E.g. I got through a long night with the baby)

_____

_____

_____

3. *What are you really good at, as a mum?*
   (E.g. Giving my baby what they need, when they
   need it)

_____

_____

_____

♡

'Support and
understanding
are the two most
important things
for a new mum'

♡

I wish I knew ...

I'd struggle to connect with my child

I really struggled to connect with Brody. People say that when you meet your baby, there'll be this instant connection. Everyone kept saying that to me, and I absolutely believed them that it would happen.

I had this in my head the whole time when I was having my caesarean. The minute I got cut open, I was lying on the bed and everyone around me said, 'You're going to get this overwhelming feeling, it's the best feeling ever.' I was waiting and waiting for that feeling to come, for the rush to happen, but it didn't. We brought Brody home and I was thinking, *This is weird.* I had lots of feelings, and it was overwhelming, but I didn't get the natural mother's instinct bond everyone told me I would get. Obviously I loved him and was so happy he was here safely, but I was waiting for that special feeling everyone had described, and I had been so excited for it to happen for me. Everyone said I would just know what to do and I would be so happy, but I didn't know what to do and I was so overwhelmed. I started to think that something was wrong with me.

When that feeling didn't happen, it completely threw me. I went through all the emotions: I was lonely, I felt sad. My house was packed with people, which I normally love, but I couldn't wait to be on my own. I don't know why I wanted that actually, because I felt so lonely. You'd have thought I'd have wanted to be with other people, but I went the opposite way and just felt really sad when surrounded by people. I couldn't understand why everyone around me was so happy, but I wasn't. I really struggled with that then. Now, looking back,

I know it's such a normal feeling. I wish I'd known just how normal it was, but how would I have known, as no one talks about it?

It was such an amazing time – I had brought a life into this world – but emotionally it was a sad time for me and so different to what I had expected. I would look at Brody, and think he was so small and so cute, but I remember thinking, *Ah, why have I not got that feeling?* I started thinking it was me and questioning if I was good enough. Maybe being a parent wasn't actually for me? I went down quite a dark spiral of thoughts, of not being good enough, of being broken in some way.

Tommy spotted it and could see quite clearly I wasn't right. One day in the middle of it all, I was downstairs with my mum, Bev, my midwife Pat and Tommy. He said, 'Georgia's not right.' And they all said, 'What?' And I burst out crying because of the relief I felt that he'd noticed. I needed someone to notice. I didn't want to say it because I felt embarrassed. It shouldn't have been embarrassing but I was ashamed to admit that I was struggling.

I felt terrible. You're made to believe that as a woman, you just get on with it, you know exactly what to do, it'll all just come naturally. But I didn't know what to do, and so I thought there was something really wrong with me.

After Tommy said that, and I burst out crying, my mum and Pat reassured me, 'It's really normal, a lot of women get like this.' They kept repeating how normal it was, and the more they were saying it, the more I got better.

I felt so lost before that. I needed someone to notice, so they could say my own feelings out loud. I couldn't. I didn't feel like myself. I didn't want to be around anyone. I'd be in the bathroom, just crying and waiting for them to go. I felt safer on my own because of that feeling of embarrassment. I didn't want to tell everyone, and I was also worried people would notice.

I shared my feelings with my friends afterwards and they said it had happened to them, too. None of them had spoken about it.

So that's what I want to do. To remind you how

it's weird we are expected to just get on with it. That we should talk about ourselves more when we have babies, not less.

'I was waiting and waiting for that feeling to come, for the rush to happen, but it didn't'

Advice for new mums:

- *Never feel embarrassed to admit you are struggling – we are only human, not robots!*

- *Take the help. If there are people offering, just say yes.*

- *Reduce the pressure you put on yourself, give yourself a break.*

- *Remember that everything is a phase, it will pass.*

- *Enjoy the downtime: listen to a podcast when you're feeding the baby, or read a book.*

- *Message people on social media who are also up with babies, so you feel less alone.*

- *It's too important not to repeat: take the help. If there are people offering, say yes.*

I wish I knew ...

Motherhood wouldn't come naturally to me

Not much of motherhood came naturally to me. I didn't try breastfeeding because I really didn't want to do it. That's all there was to it and that's more than enough of a reason. I'm glad I took that pressure off myself because I didn't need any extra pressure! Loving someone came naturally because I like looking after people, but I'd never changed a nappy or given a baby a bottle so I had to learn all of that. I didn't even want to pick up the baby at first; I was quite nervous.

I was in the hospital for two nights with Brody and the midwives would do the nappy changes and bottles. I'd just watch them. Then in the middle of the night, Brody started crying and Tommy was in another room sleeping. The midwife didn't come in so I jumped up and ran over, all secretively, and I changed his nappy on my own. It was such a big moment for me. Tommy came in and asked what I was doing and I said I'd just changed a nappy and I hadn't wanted anyone to watch me. I didn't want the midwife to see and tell me I was doing it wrong. I was embarrassed for her to know I'd never done it before. When she came in, she didn't say anything about it, of course, because it was normal. But I was so proud of myself.

The next morning, Pat – my midwife – came in and she asked if I needed any help with little things, like changing a nappy. I said I'd changed a nappy the night before and she gave me a few extra tips, like always remember to make sure the willy's down, because they'll wee on you, and she said to pull out the sides of the nappy. I look back and think, *How cute that I was so naive.* You're not supposed to know how to do absolutely everything in your life.

Remember . . .

It's OK to ask for help. I thought I was expected to know how to do everything, so I didn't want to try doing anything at first, in case I got it wrong. But you can learn from my mistake and as soon as there's something you don't know how to do, reach out and ask for support. People are there to help you. For some, it is their literal job, like a midwife or nurse or doctor, but you'll find your community in your friends and family who rally around you too. Don't be afraid to ask for their help when you need extra support.

♡

'You're not supposed to know how to do absolutely everything in your life'

♡

I wish I knew . . .

No matter what, you need support

My friends and family were amazing when I had Brody. My mum moved in with me for two weeks and Bev, Tommy's mum, was here every day. I needed that, especially after a C-section. It was new for them, being nannies, and they absolutely loved it. Everyone was here a lot but then that's what they thought I wanted – that I wouldn't have wanted an empty house.

I got all the help and support I needed because of that and I'm so thankful, because I wouldn't have got through those first few weeks without them. Tommy, my mum and Bev were just amazing. I dread to think what would have happened if I hadn't had that support. My thoughts and feelings could have spiralled. So I'm really thankful, and I know I'm lucky to have had them there.

What helped me begin to find my way was time. They say time is a healer and it really is. The mornings started getting brighter. Brody was having more sleep, I was opening up more. Everything was coming together. I'd wash my hair, and enjoy that as a little win, along with getting dressed for the day. You have to really appreciate those little things, as they're big when you're a new mum. I had days where I didn't get out of my pyjamas too and that's fine. I stopped putting pressure on myself about things like changing the nappy bin. I gave myself an easier time.

I gave myself a break.

Now look at me – at the time of writing this, I'm two years on and so connected with Brody. I know what he's thinking before he says it. I know him so well, we are the best of friends, and I'm obsessed with him. Some people get a connection with their child when they're pregnant, some people get it when the baby's born, and some people get it a few months later. Everyone's different, just like every child is different. We just need to worry about our own mental health rather than worrying about what we 'should' be doing.

Because ultimately, if you're not happy, your child's not going to be happy – so you need to look after yourself first.

The minute I began talking about my feelings and opening up, my life started coming together. It did take time, of course, it's not an overnight thing, but I think people watched me more once they knew, so they could step in and make things easier when I needed them to.

I was no longer embarrassed to say if I was struggling or tired. If I was more open, other people were more open. As the days and weeks went on, Brody got easier as he grew; I let people help me with night feeds, and stopped being so controlling. Brody started sleeping the odd night through, and then the summer came. The days began to get easier, the night feeds weren't so scary. The seasons change, whether you notice or not. Time really will heal.

What makes a good mum?

Loving your child. Wanting the best for them.

It doesn't matter what you buy them, as long as they're safe, they're fed, they're watered, clothed, comfy and loved.

That's all they need. A child just wants love and safety. Give it to them, and to me you're a good mum.

♡

'I had days where
I didn't get out of my
pyjamas and that's fine.
I stopped putting pressure
on myself. I gave myself
an easier time. I gave
myself a break'

♡

I wish I knew ...
That one day
I'd have all the courage
I'd ever need

I didn't feel courageous as a child. Deep down, whenever I had to try new things, I was always so scared because I didn't believe I could do it. I can track through my life where the same thing was happening, that fear holding me back a lot.

When I was younger, my auntie had a drama school, and one day she said I was going to get on stage and sing. I cried the day before, saying I couldn't do it. I felt sick with nerves. But I did it, and I knew I wasn't good at it. I felt awful when I was on stage and when I got off, I said to my mum,

'I'm never going back there again.' I locked myself in the toilets!

I also did a few TV adverts when I was younger. There surely must have been a bit of me that was excited and wanting to do it, while the other half was terrified.

I did quite a few of those ads. I filmed for Nickelodeon, Fox Kids, Disney. I enjoyed drama but I never thought, *I'm amazing, I'm going to be an actress.* I just did it for the fun of it, you know? I didn't take it seriously. I now know that doing those ads would have taken guts, so maybe I was more courageous than I thought.

As a child, I was scared of the usual things like spiders. But what I've always been most scared of is people leaving. At the end of the weekend when I was young, if we had friends or family round and they needed to leave, I'd start crying.

I always say now that something must've happened to me as a child. It's a joke between us all – all my family say it, and Tommy – but I've got a big thing about people leaving. If my mum's round and staying the night, the next day I'll get tearful when she leaves – even if I'm seeing her again in a few days!

I think it's because as a family, we had so many people round all the time, and I had friends round so often too. When they left, it felt so quiet. I'd feel this intense sense of loss. Having a busy house and having people around all the time is what made me happy. I still love having a packed house.

People come to my house now and say, 'Oh my god, it is so chaotic.' I'll have cleaners, a gardener, my mum, sister, Bev, parcels coming in all day, I'll be shooting content and then a friend will turn up. I can easily deal with that, I genuinely love it. Everything always seems to happen at once, people always turn up at the same time, and I thrive off that. If it's just me and Brody, sometimes I get in the weirdest mood and then have to just drive to my mum and it's all OK. Mum always had people in and out of our house, and she still lives with my brother and sister and her boyfriend, so she's still got a busy house.

At school, I had loads of friends and was genuinely

happy, but at parents' evenings, the teachers always said the same thing: 'She's her own worst enemy.' That's all I got told, so it seeped into me. I didn't know how to change it, though. I was very sociable, nice and polite, so I got away with not being so good at the academic side of things. But as soon as I got a school project, I'd panic and think I couldn't do it before I'd even started. That's what they meant by me being my own worst enemy: my fear of not being able to do something properly held me back.

I used to put my hand up a lot at school and ask lots of questions and then one day I just stopped. I was really young and I can't remember which teacher it was but this must have really affected me, because it's such a strong memory. She lifted up my work and said, 'Whose writing is this?' She was taking the piss out of the handwriting, saying it was terrible. I was so embarrassed. My mum said my writing got worse and worse after that. In fact, my writing's still terrible. It really affected my confidence, so I stopped asking so many questions, stopped working on my handwriting at all. I'm dreading Brody going to nursery because it could be anyone looking after him. I'm still affected by that and I'm thirty-two. It stays with you.

A few years ago, I developed a new fear. And it was petrifying. It came about because I'd done a show called *Coach Trip* with Tommy, where you're on a coach with all these people filming from early in the morning until late at night. I'd never ever done filming like that. It was so long. Anyway, I finished that show and then went straight on to another show and it was basically training you to swim the Channel. I have no idea why I said yes, it was mental. I remember thinking, *This isn't for me.* I don't like swimming. I'm really, really scared of swimming in the sea. I'm not a strong swimmer. I can swim in a swimming pool a little bit, but I wouldn't say I can *swim* swim. And this show was all about getting celebrities who aren't really good swimmers, and teaching them to swim well enough so that you could all swim the Channel. Wild.

I started doing the training in my dad's swimming pool, and did five weeks with a trainer. We had to do lessons every day, three times a week. So I did all of that. And then we started doing the group things and going into open water, and that's when it really hit me and I thought, *I can't fucking do this.* It was too much. But I don't know if it actually was too much, or if I was doing too much in general and I just couldn't cope. I think I needed to just not talk to anyone for a bit.

After that, I had a bit of a breakdown, I didn't know what I was doing. It all went a bit mad. I really couldn't snap out of it.

Usually, I'd hate starting a show and not finishing it, because I feel like it's embarrassing. I wouldn't want to let people down. Fortunately, the team I was with were really nice and understood. I'd done an intense series of *TOWIE*, and had loads going on with Tommy in that series; *Coach Trip* filming was full-on just before it. The only time you're not filming is when you're sleeping. Literally, even when you're eating, you're getting filmed. And I wasn't used to that. It was like being on *Big Brother*, and it was unbelievably intense.

I kept crying and crying, and was in a very dark place. I didn't know what was happening. I wasn't happy. Carrying on wasn't worth it, nothing's worth my peace. The lady who was there as a swimming coach was like, 'Georgia, it's too much for you. Just don't worry.' And when she said that, I said, 'Oh my god, yes, thank you.'

Considering I've done TV for so long, I haven't really had many periods of burnout like that. You get the odd moment when you're a bit down, because TV life is very up and down. The highs are really high, then the lows are extremely low. But that was a low that I felt like I couldn't get out of, and it's so important to have people around you in that moment who can spot it and help you see the light in the darkness.

I can now look back on my life, on all of the different things I've done, and tried – just had a go at – and think, *Yes, I have courage. I always give it a go.* My fear doesn't hold me back as much any more, and I think that's all we can ask of ourselves as we get older.

Dealing with burnout:

- *Don't ignore the warning signs. When you start to feel tired and stressed, look at what you have going on.*

- *Is there anything you can drop, stop or slow down?*

- *Who can you turn to for support?*

- *Try and take a break from your work, even if it's just for a week.*

- *Write down how you're feeling; journal it out.*

- *Keep talking. Holding it all inside won't solve anything.*

- *Go out into nature. Walking always helps.*

- *Rest, drink lots of water, eat nutritious food.*

- *Drop the guilt. If you need to say no, say no.*

♡

'What I've always
been most scared of
is people leaving'

♡

I wish I knew ...

It's important to be able to say 'no'

You've got to know what you want to do and what you don't want to do, and also what's good for you to do. You can't say yes to everything to please other people, and you can't just do things because you think it's going to look good. What do you get out of that, really?

You need to be true to yourself. If you know deep down it's not for you, then you shouldn't do it.

There is some courage in saying 'no'. And I've got really good at that now! I've got proper boundaries. I will try things, I will go for meetings, I'll meet new people to see what I think. But if there are events or jobs that don't feel right, I will always say no.

The thing is, once you start saying no, you can't stop – you carry on. It's such a powerful thing, to respect yourself, your time and effort, enough to say no.

In any job, in anyone's life, if something makes you feel uncomfortable or destroys your peace, it's not worth it. You are allowed to say no. Regardless of what level you start at or where you are, there should be boundaries in anything you do. You don't have to wait until you're at breaking point.

I think that to be successful, you have to say no to things. You can't take it all on. If you said yes all the time to everything, you would be drained. Tommy's always been good at saying no, and has built an empire because of it.

He has a really clear vision and stays on his path. He doesn't take on other people's problems. So if someone says, 'I really want you to come to this,' he's like, 'If I can't do it, I can't do it, so no thank you.' He doesn't feel bad about it because it is the truth of it all. If someone expected me to go to an event just because they're holding it – well, I'd probably say, 'I've got to go to that.' But Tommy will be like, 'Why? We haven't got to do anything.' And it's so refreshing. Because he's right.

Maybe men find that easier – saying no – because I think as women, we're expected to be open, to be people pleasers, to make everyone's lives easier. Now I've got Brody, I have to put extremely firm boundaries in place, because if something affects me, it affects my child. If I'm not 100 per cent me, then it affects him.

Brody has helped me to have firmer boundaries. Having him has changed the way I think; the way I do things. It's given me more courage to say no as well, because I'm protecting him. When you're talking for that person, when you're their voice because they are younger, the no's are so easy!

Filming my show *Baby Steps* works well around motherhood. The team know that if I'm booked in to film and Brody just wants me, I'm not doing it. It is what it is! My child needs me, so therefore I am there for him. Before, I'd have been terrified to let people down, but when it comes to Brody, I'll let anyone down. I don't care one bit. Even if I was booked in to meet the King, if Brody wanted me, I'd say, 'Sorry, I can't come.' I'm so thankful that this is my job because there are so many roles where it doesn't work like that at all.

Creating boundaries:

- *When someone asks you to go to or do something, whether it's an event, or a job at work, take stock first of how it feels in your body.*

- *Does your body feel energised, excited, do you have butterflies?*

- *Or do you feel low, flat, panicked and stressed?*

- *Pay attention to those signs; that's your intuition guiding you in the right direction.*

- *If it feels good, maybe give it a try. If it doesn't, politely decline.*

- *Notice how good it feels, having said no.*

♡

'You need to be
true to yourself.
If you know deep down
it's not for you, then
you shouldn't do it'

♡

I wish I knew ...
It's good to
leave your comfort zone

Even though I say no a lot, I still push myself out of my comfort zone. My team have brought up the prospect of me going on a certain show on ice, and it feels like the scariest job that I could ever be put forward for! The thought of actually standing on ice freaks me out! This year, after three years of having conversations, I've agreed to go for the meeting. (I did try to get out of it but you know me now – I've agreed to do it, so I'll do it.)

Still, I'm messaging my agent saying, 'I don't know if I can do it, I'm really scared.' And she's like, 'Georgia, you'll be fine.' It's an unknown. But to try and calm myself, I thought, *Well, what could happen? I could fall on the ice. That's really it, isn't it?* And when you think through the scenarios like that, it makes it much easier to just to say yourself: *OK, maybe I'll just do it.* So I'm going to just see what happens.

I could really enjoy it as well! That's what the fear never takes into account, and that's why I'm going, because there are other thoughts in my head saying, *Maybe it'd be good for you, or even if you don't get it, maybe it will lead to something else.* I've got to stop letting the fear take over.

I overthink things massively, even things like nice events I'm invited to. I'll say, 'Oh, I don't think I can go,' and then my agent will say, 'You're fine, you've got a week's notice, you're fine.' I have to know what I'm doing. I'm not good at last-minute stuff.

With people coming round to my house, I'm happy for the spontaneity; people just rocking up. But when it comes to work events, they all need to be planned. I think it's because home is my safety net. When you leave and you're going to events or jobs, I need to think about things in minute detail. All the questions – what am I going to do? Who will I talk to? What will I wear? – become so big in my head. Since having Brody, it scares me more leaving home now, or going out for a job.

I've lost myself in this new job, of motherhood and raising Brody. But you have to put yourself out there again.

As a mother, you've got more to think about. Before having a kid, it's just about you. Now there's part of me that wants to do more for Brody – more jobs, earn more money, show him what I can do. I'm working on finding the right balance.

Five steps to stretching your comfort zone:

1. *Name one thing firmly in your comfort zone.*

2. *Name one thing at the edges of your comfort zone.*

3. *Name one thing way out of your comfort zone.*

4. *Challenge yourself to give 2 and 3 a go.*

5. *How does it feel, stretching your comfort zone in this way?*

♡

'I've got to stop
letting the fear
take over'

♡

I wish I knew ...
That fad diets
don't work

I had a good relationship with my body as a child. I never had any issues, I thought I was just pretty normal. I remember my friends saying that I had long legs and thinking, *Is that a good thing?*

I had my boobs done when I was twenty-one. I always knew I was going to get my nose and boobs done. I felt like my body was fine in general, but I had bigger boobs and as I started getting a bit older, I realised that the shape wasn't quite right. They were quite pointy, and one was pointier than the other. I didn't really realise until I got to my late teens. I was putting on a bikini, and the bikini top had little triangles, and I remember putting it on and thinking, *This boob looks different to that boob.* I started looking, and once you notice it, you can't un-notice. I did loads of research before getting my boobs done as it's a big decision, but I knew it was right for me. I'm glad I made that decision.

With my nose, I grew up knowing I'd have it done. My mum and all my aunties had theirs done. Even my dad! Well, he broke his nose, and to fix it they had to basically give him a nose job. So, I grew up in a house where everyone had had it done. Weirdly, when I was young, it didn't bother me. I was never bullied for it or anything. It didn't start to bother me until I got into my twenties. And it bothered me when I was on TOWIE because I was having to watch myself on TV.

My mum and dad had both said to me, 'Wait to do your nose.' So I did wait. And I'm glad I did, because I might have otherwise rushed into it and gone to a random surgeon who wasn't that confident . . . Your nose changes with your face as you get older, so I don't think you should rush something like that. Getting my boobs done was scary, but it wasn't a massive deal, because you can't see them, only I can. Your nose is quite different, though!

I don't think I had ever really thought about my body properly until I joined TOWIE. I never had a problem weight-wise. I never thought about it in a negative way, or about dieting. I just ate what I wanted to. I was pretty active too. But when I joined TOWIE, it all changed. Until then, I always felt like I was slim, but suddenly, everyone else was slimmer, and I realised very quickly that the slimmer girls would get more work, and they'd get more press and more articles. I became obsessed, and I became really, really slim. Too skinny.

I did any diet I could find. Every diet. I did diet pills, every one you could imagine. I did juice diets . . . Anything I could get my hands on, I would do. I would've done anything just to be skinny, and I'd do all the diets and pills at the same time. I'd get ideas from my friends, or from what I was hearing about on the grapevine. I'd be going to the gym twice a day. It was excessive.

When I look back now, my calorie intake was ridiculous. I was not consuming what I should have been consuming to live a normal life. I got so skinny that I actually blacked out in the gym once. I went home and told my mum what had happened, and she said, 'You need to stop this,' and really went in on me. And I did stop. I stopped being as obsessed.

I really loved being thin. Imagine you're twenty-two or twenty-three, and you've got a camera on you in a bikini, and paps constantly stalking you. It's a lot for a young girl. So I had to make sure that I looked amazing in a bikini. I made sure that I was the one that was 'the best girl in the bikini'. Because everyone on TOWIE had their thing, and I thought, OK, *that's my thing now.* I mean, it's mental, not least because everyone looked so good that competing in that way was daft anyway.

I remember turning up one year to a TOWIE shoot, and the exec and everyone said, 'Oh my god, you look so good.' That made me carry on. I thought, *This is good for me. I'm getting the attention I need.* Then came the articles about having the best body on the show. Whoever got the *Daily Mail* headline was winning. I mean, it's pathetic, but back then it felt important, like a way to be judged the best: the winner of a contest that feels very real when you're in newspapers and magazines.

With that TOWIE life – where you're filming one minute, then you're completely out of the limelight – I ended up creating a cycle of on and off dieting. I realised that I could eat a bit more when I was in the off cycle, not filming, and then I started eating actual food, and realised that carbs weren't the enemy, and that they give you more energy to go to the gym. So I developed a healthy approach to eating and working out.

After I left TOWIE back in 2021, it was really refreshing to not worry about it as much. That's why I think I loved being pregnant so much, because I didn't have to worry about my body. It had a new role. I could relax.

I'll never forget that one of my first-ever big marketing campaigns I did was with a bread company. I really, really wanted to do it because

I'd learnt so much since my TOWIE days, and I desperately wanted to put that out there – that food isn't the enemy. I did that campaign twice, and they even won an award for it! I wanted young girls to know that you don't need to do all those stupid things, like cut out carbs for years. Eat the bread!

I think my obsession with being thin was partly from TOWIE and wanting to be the best, but I know I also liked being able to control it. When I look back, maybe that was the only thing at the time I *could* control – my mum and dad started separating and I had my shop, which was growing. I had so much going on that was out of my control, but something I could control was what I was eating and how I looked.

In terms of media pressure, I don't think it came from them. I was excited to be getting the coverage, and that was part of my job. I think the pressure was more from within. I'd look at the other girls on TOWIE, and I'd think, *That's who I want to be. I need to look like them.* The competitiveness didn't really affect our relationships. We all got on. (Well, we all had our moments.) But we were all doing the same thing, I think, deep down, wondering, *Who's going to look the best?*

Outside of TOWIE, with my old friends, everyone wanted to look good but we weren't competing at all. I would look at it as, *That's my job.* And you get taken more seriously if you look the best. Back in the day, if you looked good in a bikini, you'd get more clothing jobs, you'd get more brands hiring you to promote their stuff. You knew that your job was to look good and the better you looked, the more work you'd get. So it becomes a cycle, doesn't it? And then you're more popular and become more involved in the TOWIE chats and the scenes, and as you do more scenes, you become more popular. It was a cycle really.

I think nowadays I wouldn't have got away with being so obsessed with my weight – it would have been picked up on. I was lucky my mum was always onto me so it didn't become a problem. If I hadn't had my mum backing me, I could have potentially got a lot worse. Because the thing is, if you get so obsessed with something, so consumed, you don't know what can happen, do you?

I felt really free when I was pregnant. Wearing a tight dress and showing my belly off felt lovely, because to do that normally, I'd feel like I had to train and make sure I was spending a lot of time in the gym to be wearing a tight outfit or to have a crop top on. Being pregnant was the first time I ever felt like, *Wow, I can be in a tight dress* and *I can eat what I want*, and I loved it.

I wasn't bothered about comparing myself to the other TOWIE women at all at that point. I was like, *Yep, you've got a four-pack, and that's lovely, and I have a bump which I love so much.* That's when I completely changed my whole outlook on what makes me happy. I think that's why I left TOWIE as well. I was offered my own show, which made the decision easier, but I had grown as a person too. I was so much more relaxed and I started thinking, *I'm not bothered that that person slagged that person off. I can't be bothered to get involved.* In my early twenties, I was involved in everyone's business. I would be the first to stand up for a friend if someone said something behind their back. I'd be the first to out them or stick up for someone. I was always the mediator. When I got pregnant, I realised, *No, I'm not doing that. It's just not me any more.*

Tommy loved my pregnant body too, which definitely helped. After giving birth, I looked in the mirror and thought, *What the fuck is that?* I was shocked because I thought everyone's belly's shrunk back down immediately after the baby came out. Everyone had said, 'You'll bounce back,' and I thought they meant literally! But I still looked pregnant. I very much looked pregnant coming out of the hospital, which is completely normal, I now know. But I didn't know then because no one is open about this side of it.

I remember seeing a photo a few months later of a celebrity who'd had a baby around the same time I had Brody and she'd put a picture up of her six-pack. I thought, *What the fuck?* I was in such a weird place with my hormones all over the shop and then you've got all this 'get your body back' stuff to contend with.

It really threw me back to that time I was twenty-two, because I thought, *Why don't I look like that? Why am I not like that?* And then one day it clicked for me: *Fuck this. I've just grown a baby. I've been cut open to deliver this baby safely. I've got this beautiful child and I'm worried about a belly?* So I sent Tommy a picture of my postnatal belly, still looking pregnant, and I said, 'Should I put this up?' He messaged back immediately, saying, '100 per cent'. That's the support I needed.

I was really nervous but I put the picture of me with my belly out on Instagram and did a big rant and, do you know what? It was really empowering and inspired me. Loads of other women said it helped them as well. That was a big moment. When I put that picture up, it changed the game for me. So many people loved it and said they felt seen, and I loved seeing people post similar pictures after that.

When I had Brody, I started doing things that I hadn't seen anyone else I follow do before. There were posts I wanted to be seeing but wasn't seeing on my feed, so I decided to brave it and share my reality. It was scary, but I've always had an open approach to motherhood. I say it how I see it – and that's what I needed more than ever once I became a mum. For myself, and for others, to see normality. That's how I've grown an amazing community on Instagram.

If I'm being honest, though, I do remember thinking after I posted the picture of my belly, *I might not get any brand deals or other jobs now because everyone knows I look like that.* And then I thought, *What am I talking about?* It's just the way we've been taught to think – that our bodies equal our worth. And the truth is, I've got so many brand deals off the back of being honest about how I look and feel as a mother. I ended up getting all the jobs I ever wanted. All of them. If you're true to yourself and you're your own cheerleader, you get what you deserve.

I'm grateful that Tommy has always backed me and doesn't add any pressure, especially in terms of body image. I was just trying to survive. The gym wasn't on my calendar at all. I would go on walks but my priority wasn't to lose weight. My priority was to raise a child and keep him alive and keep myself alive.

Now Brody is a bit older, I'm in a weird place. I lost a baby in summer 2023, and when I was pregnant, I gained so much weight. I was eating a lot more. I think because it was such a stressful thing from the minute I got pregnant.

I do that. I'm an emotional eater, so I'll eat with emotions. I didn't care about the weight gain, though, because I was pregnant, and obviously the only thing I cared about was keeping this baby alive. And then when it didn't work out, in my head I was still pregnant. I was still eating like I was pregnant. I was pregnant for four months and when I lost the baby, I still had a bit of a bump.

I've struggled to lose that bump. I'm not wanting to lose it, because I want to be pregnant again.

I've started trying to set my mind up to be healthier now.

Before, what was happening was that I wasn't eating breakfast and then I'd be starving, so when

I saw Brody had left three slices of toast, I'd eat them up. Then I'd think, *Oh, there's some crisps, I'll have them too.* Soon, I realised I might as well have eaten a whole meal, because I'd picked at all that food anyway. I'm not doing that any more, and I take each day as it comes. It's hard to break years of conditioning on how we think of our bodies as women, and take the time to figure out what we really need. I want to get pregnant again, and have a wedding to plan for next year. So, here's to future me liking what she sees in the mirror, because she's happy with life, not just her body.

'Eat the bread!'

How to cultivate a healthier relationship with your body:

- *Be active. It feels good to exercise, especially if you do it for how it feels rather than because you want to lose weight.*

- *Eat whatever you like, in moderation. No food is bad; I love my McDonald's, but I try to eat healthily most of the time so I can then really enjoy treats.*

- *Don't compare yourself to other people. There will always be someone thinner, more toned, with a better tan. Look at what you've got, rather than what they have.*

- *Enjoy your body changing in pregnancy. You're growing a baby! What could be more amazing than that? It's well worth the extra fat and stretch marks.*

- *Wear clothes that feel comfortable in the postnatal period. Don't worry about getting back into your old jeans. Take your time to recover.*

- *You're doing a great job.*

I wish I knew . . .

What relationships are really like

I'd never met anyone like Tommy when we first got together, ever. He was really loud; very in your face! I remember thinking, *I want to know who this person is.*

I'd never dated someone on the same TV show as me, so it was scary to think our relationship was about to be played out on the telly. My ex-boyfriend was the complete opposite of Tommy: he was really quiet and had a normal job. He didn't get my TV career, but I felt safe in that relationship because it was familiar, and private. With Tommy, I thought, *Oh my god, it's on TV, everyone's going to be commenting on it.* How would it be personal in any way? Everyone would have something to say and know your business.

I was with my ex for about four years and we split up a few months before I got together with Tommy. Tommy was so unexpected for me. To be honest, I thought it was going to be more of a holiday thing! Turns out, we would never leave each other's side. I didn't really have any time in between relationships to think properly about what I wanted. Tommy came in, bam, done.

When Tommy joined TOWIE, I was already on it. He joined when we were doing summer in Ibiza and I was fuming. I'd been talking to him just before I left, and he told me he was going to Dubai. I didn't really want to talk to him any more then because I thought, *There's no point, if you're going to live in Dubai.* And then he turned up on TOWIE and I thought, *I don't like you any more because you've lied.* He just thought it was funny, pranking me. I didn't speak to him for two days. And then after that, we became literally inseparable. I got home from TOWIE, met his mum and thought, *Shit, we're going to be together, aren't we?*

Obviously, we went through loads of stuff because we were on TOWIE; we were two young people and he was a bit of a party boy. But we ended up doing it properly. We're still together now, nine years down the line.

I think we're a good match because we balance each other out. We're alike in some ways but then we are polar opposites in others, which is interesting. If I was like him, we wouldn't be able to be together and vice versa. I'm laidback and he's not. You always need that one person to calm the other down.

We're alike in our values too. We both grew up with low self-belief. When we spoke about things in the early days, just as we were getting together, we realised we were very similar. We didn't know where we fitted in or know what we wanted to do. Tommy knew he loved trainers and wanted to get into that in some way, so he did have a passion, whereas I didn't. So work-wise we're the complete opposite, because he is a go-getter and I'm a bit more of a plodder. I'm more of a home person, whereas he wants to be travelling all the time. But we balance each other out. As we all know, opposites attract.

Tommy and I had a really tough patch. In 2022, we were on the verge of splitting up. And I remember saying, 'Love's not enough to keep this working.' We just weren't getting on, we were at loggerheads all the time, we were thinking of things really differently. We were clashing over stupid things and in the end it was so draining that I thought, *I can't do this.* And he said, 'I can't do it either.' We didn't want to split up because we've got Brody. It would have been the absolute worst thing. It's the last thing you want to do when you become a mum. We went through a really shit time. I was aware that something wasn't right because he would be triggered by the most random stuff. And I'd think, *Why would that bother you?*

He'd be annoyed by a loud noise. A dog bark would trigger him. The baby crying would trigger him. It felt like something was heightened in his brain; something wasn't right. I remember I was in the car and I plucked up the courage to ring him. I think it's easier to have those kinds of conversations over the phone. I said, 'I think you need to get tested. I think you need to go to someone and get tested for ADHD or something.'

And he agreed, which I was really shocked about. He booked the appointment and they said he had severe ADHD. They actually said, 'I don't know how you've got through life without knowing.'

I don't know where I'd got the idea that he might have ADHD. I'd started googling what he was doing, his symptoms, and it all kept coming back to ADHD. All of these webpages sounded like they were describing Tommy. Once he went and got the assessment, he went on medication and then things started to get better. It happened quite quickly. Well, quicker than I expected it to change.

It went from both of us looking at different places to live, with all the family involved, to being able to talk about things, open up and try to be on the same page again.

That's why I'm a really big advocate for medication, if you need it and have had the time to know if you really need it. If Brody was diagnosed and really needed it, now I wouldn't say no, because I've lived through the consequences of someone with severe ADHD living without medication and it's really tough. I feel like Tommy was just waiting for someone to pinpoint it, and I'm so glad we did.

I never get bored with Tommy because there's always something going on in our life. It's never been a nine-to-five normal life that I live, ever. I think I like it like that, but then I don't know any different.

When I'm older I might want something different. When I'm really, really old, I'll probably just want to be in Spain on the beach, living my life by the sea.

Now, I feel like we've still got loads to do, and I don't see Tommy slowing down ever. He'll have a walking stick and still be on it.

Even though we're very different, I do think we're a good team. We've been through difficult things together, experiences that most other couples haven't. We're stronger. And you have to be a good team to survive life with children!

Remember . . .

Most couples go through tricky patches. There are
so many different factors that can cause a wedge.
It might be money, trust issues, secrecy or – as was
the case with us – there might be an undiagnosed
neurodivergence that needs looking into. The
two most important things in a relationship are to
keep the communication open – don't bottle up
the issues, ever – and to be kind to each other.
Remember, you're in it for the long haul. If you want
to grow old together, you'll need to give each other
a bit of leeway.

♡

'I remember thinking,
I want to know
who this person is'

♡

I wish I knew ...
Everything's a compromise

♡

Everything's a compromise. That's a fact.

We went to Spain for five weeks in summer 2023. I didn't know if I could do it for that long, but Tommy said, 'Just go with this.' It was a big deal for me, going for so long. I was leaving behind my friends and family who I love being with and see most days. I'm a proper homebody and I like my routines, so it meant stepping out of my comfort zone. It sounds mad to some people, they're like: 'Why would you *not* want to go to Spain for five weeks?' But that's just me. Tommy thrives on being in Spain, just the three of us, but then he's more introverted and I'm more extroverted. I like having all my people around me. So that's a compromise I made for him and I enjoyed it in the end.

Tommy is different to me in that he likes peace and quiet, and having fewer people around. He's more sociable now and he's getting used to having a house full of people all the time but before, it would feel like more of a clash rather than compromise because he didn't want people around him much at all. There's things that he will do or say and I have to really take a deep breath before I react and think, OK, *it's because he thinks slightly differently to me.* And that's what I'm learning to do.

Even though Tommy feels uncomfortable in certain situations, he's started going along with them more, and making compromises for me. Even things like Brody's parties. I throw massive parties! I've thrown two big parties that would normally freak him out, but he shows up and he's part of it. And even hosting events at our house and with filming stuff, he's getting used to all of it.

We should probably do more just the two of us, but we don't because our house is always full.

Our lives are quite hectic, but we do commit to little dates, like we'll just go to get breakfast or we'll get a bit of dinner, or go for a little drive if one of the nans are OK to look after Brody. We've got no problem asking them for help because they love him as much as we do – if not more!

'Remember: you're in it together'

Remember . . .

- *All relationships involve some compromise.*

- *It's good to sometimes push yourself out of your comfort zone.*

- *Get clear on what's non-negotiable for you and share this with your partner.*

- *Also, ask them what their non-negotiables are and try to respect that.*

- *Come up with a plan together for dealing with the things you each find hard.*

- *Remember: you're in it together.*

I wish I knew ...

That hairspray gets rid of stains on sofas

I discovered this after Brody drew on the sofa. (Why would you draw on the sofa? There are walls! Or even better, paper!) I was so stressed.

I panicked and nearly stuck the covers in the washing machine. But you don't! You spray the mark with hairspray and then you get a damp cloth, rub it, and it comes off. You're welcome.

When it comes to mess from having a baby, I choose my battles. There are times in the day when I think, *Do I tidy up all of his toys or just leave them? Once he gets up from his nap, he's going to do it again.* I don't stress over it. At the end of the day, he's a baby and he's playing. But if I've got visitors, I do like to clean the kitchen. I'm not really bothered about the rest of the house, but as long as in the kitchen the milk's put away, the sides are clean – that'll do.

If you come round to my house, you'll see the washing hanging out. I'm not going to hide that because you're coming to visit! I might put it in the utility room, but that's life and when you've got a child you're constantly washing.

Growing up, our house was always clean. My mum loved a bit of bleach! But I was never scared to get my toys out. I want Brody to be relaxed, which he definitely is. And when he goes to bed, I tidy up his toys and we start again the next day.

I always use a bit of Fairy up liquid, as I call it, on stains. I get the item and then a bit of Fairy up liquid, put it on the stain, leave it for about five minutes, scrub it off and then get the Vanish. You need it when you've got a two-year-old. Brody won't wear bibs, so I've just got to try and get all the stains out. There was a time when he was little when he shat through his whole outfit. I washed it with Fairy up liquid, put it in the sun and it was back to white in no time. Magic.

Remember . . .

A house should be lived in, not pristine. Obviously, we all like it when it's clear and clean but children properly shake things up. So let your children play; let them have fun. Take a deep breath in, sigh it out and say, 'What will be, will be. We'll clean up later.' And make yourself a nice cup of tea.

♡

'Why would you
draw on the sofa?
There are walls!'

♡

I wish I knew . . .
That living life true to you is the best way to be

On TOWIE, if Tommy and I had rowed, or had things going on, I'd always protect him and he'd always protect me. We'd always hide if we had a row, because we got burnt when we were younger as someone heard us and it became a cast problem. Everyone would comment on it and get involved. So, we quickly learnt to disguise things and I learnt how to deflect what was going on in my life, and put the attention onto other people. I became the mediator and I would always be the person who was there for other people. It meant that no one would ask what was going on in my life. I was really good at that.

I never told anyone when my mum and dad were splitting up; no one ever knew when I was younger. When me and Tom rowed, no one would ever know. I found it easier that way because I wanted to protect people around me. And I'd become really good at it. I'd always ask how people were, so no one would really know about me. But now on my show – and since I've become a mum – everything's out there, and it's refreshing.

It was hard keeping all of our arguments secret. Tommy and I would have an argument and then we'd be in a scene together and I'd still hate him, but have to act like I didn't. I knew if I showed weakness in our relationship, people would jump on it and it would become a bigger thing, a plot point for the show. And to be honest, that's what saved us. I really believe that's how we got through reality TV together, because no other couple survived it. No one. There's not one other couple I know that survived TOWIE.

It became an us against them situation! After we first got together and once we became properly united, that was it: we were a team and no one was getting in the way. I carried that on and would do it in my normal life as well. You'd get snippets in the show of me breaking down or being a bit upset because it had all become too much. Generally, though, I'm very good at deflecting.

I remember all the cast on TOWIE getting annoyed, because they would always say, 'Why do Georgia and Tommy get to talk about other people's problems and be in all of these scenes and not bring their own stuff in front of the camera?' And I'd be like, 'It's because I'm clever.' At the end of the day, the producers knew that we were giving a lot and getting involved anyway, so we didn't have to play our relationship out on camera in detail. I'd always be really good in scenes and make sure I was really giving my opinions and getting involved and helping people, so I didn't have to bring my own stuff.

We've gone from one extreme to the other now! On my show, I had Brody, filmed my whole pregnancy, then started filming again four days after giving birth. We've gone through having a baby, sharing the ADHD stuff, and also some really hard things, including losing a baby. I think that because it's our own show, we feel safe. We didn't want other people butting in like in the TOWIE days, making situations worse, or harder, so now we can be ourselves and put our lives and feelings out there.

In fact, it helps because it puts us both in awkward positions to talk about things we wouldn't normally talk about. It's therapy for us. Whereas before, we didn't need that. We just needed to protect each other. There were too many cast members getting involved and they all had something to say, and then a little issue became a bigger one. We saw couples break up on the show all the time, so we decided, 'We're not doing that.'

It's scary, though, when you start opening up together, because we tend to be filming in real-time. The ADHD episodes were filmed slightly after the events had happened, so it was easier to manage for Tommy's mental health and well-being, whereas what happened with losing the baby was being filmed literally as it was happening. It was really hard to go through but at the same time, it felt right. We promised to do this show if we could be open and honest and completely ourselves. I can't preach that and not practise it too.

If I know I'm helping someone, anyone – just one person – it gives me this power to carry on. Sometimes I think that things happen to me because I was put here to help people, be the voice that will tell it like it is, be the one that stands up for things, the person that does scary things, because it does help. I think that's given me a bit of clarity. It gives me a reason for doing what I'm doing.

How to be true to yourself:

- *If you find yourself putting on an act around certain friends, ask yourself why. What would happen if you stopped?*

- *Do you really want people in your life who you can't be fully yourself around?*

- *Focus your time and energy on friendships with people who celebrate you just as you are.*

- *Be open and vulnerable and see how people respond. Usually, they will open up to you as well and you can build a deeper connection.*

- *If there are people who want you to be someone else, wave goodbye to them. You are you. Take it or leave it. They're not worth your time.*

♡

'I'd always protect him
and he'd always
protect me'

♡

I wish I knew ...
That asking questions is OK

I always struggled with asking questions. I felt embarrassed to ask them at school in class. But knowledge is power. So don't be afraid to ask questions if you don't know something, because we're not all supposed to know what we're doing. It's OK to ask for help.

I was nervous to ask how to change a nappy after I had Brody, and how to prepare a bottle, but not asking was stupid really, because I needed to know! My auntie Sharon, my mum's sister, says I used to ask her so many questions when I was younger and she'd encourage it, which is how it should be. I was always shown that to ask questions is a sign of being interested, in wanting to learn more, or properly. But then, at school, it became almost embarrassing to admit you didn't know something. You do need confidence to put your hand up and ask questions but you should feel able to do it. If you don't, it's not your fault.

(Sometimes I do ask silly questions, but that's most of us, isn't it? Or is it just me . . .)

I'm a good listener, an understanding one, but probably not as good now; since having Brody, my brain is a bit more 'tick tock'. I'm trying to listen to whoever is speaking but I'm also thinking, *Is there something else I need to be doing? What's next on the list?*

Remember . . .

Asking questions is a good thing because it's how you learn. If anyone makes you feel uncomfortable about not already knowing something, remind them that there are many things they don't know either, and that's fine. We all start somewhere.

♡

'To ask questions
is a sign of
being interested'

♡

I wish I knew ...

Just how much your own upbringing affects the way you parent

I was born in the Essex town of Chigwell on 20 June 1991 and I had the best childhood. We lived in Chigwell – Mum and Dad, me, my sister and brother. I was the eldest and had time with my parents before my sister came along. I was so happy when she was born, though. She was like my own little doll to play with. My mum said she had to go out and buy me an actual doll and pram because sometimes, I'd get jealous of my mum pushing my sister around. When Mum would feed my sister Grace, I'd feed my 'baby' too. If I felt included, I was fine. But I'd had four and a half years with all the attention in the family and I thought I was the queen, so there were going to be some adjustments.

I remember being happy. I don't remember all that much, but I know I was happy. We had a lovely childhood home. My dad worked really hard converting a house when it was just him and my mum and when they moved in, my mum got pregnant with me straight away. It was very quick. It became the house that everyone would come to. All my friends were always round, everyone would congregate there. Everyone came over for Christmas. My house is like that now too; I've brought that with me into my own life. Saturday night Chinese at my house is a tradition, it's like a part of my DNA. When I was young, we'd have gatherings with all my mum's friends and their kids.

But while it was pretty idyllic when I was growing up, later it all went wrong.

My dad bought a massive house in the middle of nowhere, with fifteen acres of land. It was really old and we lived in that house while they converted a barn in the garden. The house was crazy. All the floors were wonky, and you'd open doors that revealed secret staircases. It had been owned by a famous musician who built the house to create accommodation for his students who'd live there. You couldn't do that these days, it'd be a bit weird, but back in the day he supposed you could. When we arrived, the land was completely overgrown and my dad had a big job to do. So, when the barn was ready, we moved in there and Dad knocked the old house down and built from the basement level up. He's not a builder, he's a property developer, but he's always very hands-on. It took years, though. Builders messed up or they'd walk off jobs.

In the end, the stress of general life, plus the build, got too much and my parents ended up splitting up. Note to self: never build a house. Joking aside, though, it became a stressful environment, and I would never want my children to live through that. It was a nightmare. I was older so I witnessed it all up close and became the mediator. I always see the best of both sides, that's a natural part of my character, and I take on people's problems. But you shouldn't be the mediator for your parents. It even put me off marriage entirely. I thought, *What's the point?* I didn't understand how you could be so happy for so long and then have it all end, just like that. My parents were the parents you never thought would break up; all my friends were so shocked.

When you've lived through a tricky divorce like that, though, it's in you, it becomes part of you. It went on and on and it built me up to become much more guarded as a person.

I became cautious. I'd never build a house with Tommy now; I'm scarred. When people say it's one of their dreams, building their own house, I say, 'Don't do it.'

I love people who are go-getters and want to earn loads of money and want to do well for their kids, but you have to remember you can't buy back time you've lost. I think that's a valuable lesson I've learnt from my childhood. Maybe that's why I'm laidback now. I like a bit of money, of course, but I'm happy with what I've got. I could probably earn much more if I had more drive, but I've been jaded by seeing what happened to my own family due to that drive to build more.

I don't want what happened to my mum and dad to happen to me and Tommy. When I met Tommy, I had to restructure my thoughts around marriage, telling myself it's nice to do, that it joins people together. And it was when I had Brody that I really thought, *OK, I get why you get married.* You become an official unit, I think.

Tommy is very driven. People say you go for people like your dad (which is a weird concept anyway) and that worries me, so I have talks with Tommy, saying, 'Please, remember what you've already got.' If you always strive for more, it will never be enough. If you're always looking for happiness, then you're not ever happy.

That said, Tommy's the most driven person I've met in my life; I've never met anyone like him. He had a different upbringing to me. In fact, his upbringing was quite similar to my dad's. They then both had to fight for what they want in life and build their empires from scratch. There are so many positives to that – my dad worked so hard to achieve all that he did; Tommy does too, but the negative side to it is that there's a tendency to always want 'more' rather than appreciating what you've already got.

How you've been brought up massively affects you as a person. You're a certain way because of it all. I love that Tommy wants more for us, and for Brody – I think that's lovely, I really do. But I also want us to keep a check on what we've got, and be thankful for it. Hopefully raising Brody with these opposing views will make him a more balanced and rounded human being.

I think we're doing a good job with Brody, he's so polite. I think every parent says that, but Brody is such a people person. He waves at everyone, high-fives them. He's not at nursery yet but he walks around saying hi to everyone, thanking cars for stopping when we cross the road. Tommy and I do clash, because Tommy was raised to believe you should be a bit 'hard'. He was raised in Islington and saw a lot more than I did; I was cushioned and protected. Tommy used to laugh at me and say I wasn't very streetwise, but I think I am now because I've been with him. He's more into tough love, but I think that just because Brody's a boy; it doesn't mean we need to instil a toughness into him.

'I thought I was
the queen, so there
were going to be some
adjustments . . .'

Remember . . .

- *Take what your parents taught you and use it wisely.*

- *You don't have to do everything your parents did.*

- *Take the bits that worked, and change the bits that don't.*

- *Tweak it for your own family.*

- *Create your own way of doing things.*

I wish I knew . . .

Mental health can affect anyone and everyone

I started getting panic attacks around the time I became really skinny, in my early twenties. Mum and Dad were splitting up; I'd met Tommy. That was a mix of really good times and also really bad. I was experiencing severe panic attacks and I didn't know anything about mental health back then. I didn't know the panic attacks were linked to my feelings of anxiety. They got so bad that I would try and climb out of the window for air.

I stopped drinking alcohol at one point, too, because if I thought about what was going on in my head, it would send me over the edge. I'd become unsociable and then Tommy and I would row because he wouldn't understand what was going on with me – but no one got it. I didn't know what was happening. But I knew if I drank, it would make it worse.

I used to get that feeling of anxiety and plan exit routes out of places. It was a really bad time. I never understood it properly until later on. Over the next few years, anxiety would pop up. Eventually, I noticed a pattern. If I was stressed or anxious, and there were big things happening, I'd get panic attacks. I then started seeing the TOWIE psychologist for it, and they helped me and gave me some great breathing techniques.

I realised then that I really needed to take care of myself. You can't ignore things. Maybe having a panic attack is my body's way of saying, 'You need to talk about things; not talking is making it all build up.'

I had therapy for ages. It was just me, talking about myself, because I never did. I got to release all of it. I stopped when I was about to have Brody, when I got pregnant. TOWIE were really good and would always say at the end of a series, 'Do you need to talk to anyone?'

When I began to get panic attacks, I started training in the gym as it used to help. On one trip, TOWIE even organised for the hotel we were staying in to open the gym early for me so I could train in the morning before my scene.

I haven't had therapy for a good couple of years now, and I think maybe I should go back, have a recap. On TOWIE, I had the show therapist, but I didn't have another one outside of the show; I didn't really need one because Tommy was my therapist. My mum was my therapist, Bev was too, and the midwife. A therapist, to me, is just someone that doesn't judge you and you can be fully open and honest with.

I've had a couple of panic attacks since Brody was born, but they've not been too bad. I had them when I lost the baby. Tom and I went away on our own for a few days to Mallorca. I started getting them out of nowhere. I don't know if it's because

I was going back to Mallorca and that's where I was when I found out I was pregnant. I haven't had one since.

Back in the TOWIE days, Tommy really learnt how to look after me. He would randomly say, 'Oh, look, there's a bottle here . . .' and would start reading a label and be like, 'Oh my god, do you know that there's this in this?' And I'd be like, 'What?' He'd take my mind off it.

Normally what happens is I get really hot and then I get a claustrophobic feeling. Then it comes over me. Once you're in it, you have to ride the wave, which is the worst bit. But I used to get it really, really bad, to the point where the panic attacks would last for so long that afterwards I'd feel like I'd been hit by a bus. I would be so worn out. They were so traumatic. Whereas now, they're not so deep. I get myself out of it before it happens.

Tommy will open the window and say, 'Right, just breathe. Do your breathing.' Then I'll say, 'Oh yeah, yeah, breathing.' You just need to remember to breathe.

Tommy's very, very intuitive. He's very spiritual. He used to talk to spirits when he was six. He gets messages come to him all the time. He's mad. I'll be lying in bed and he'll say to me, 'Stop thinking about the baby tonight.' And I'll be like, 'Oh my god, how did you know?' It's a bit annoying as well because I can't get away with anything. I can have a really bad or overwhelming day, and he'll call me and say, 'Are you all right?'

He's like that with other people, too, but he's definitely most in tune with me. My friend came around the other day. Her dad died of lung cancer when she was young. Tommy kept coming in the room where we were chatting, going, 'Amy, your dad liked football?' She said, 'Yeah, he did.' He said, 'There a shirt in a frame?' She said, 'Yeah, it's in the garage. My mum took it off the wall and put it in the garage.' He said, 'Yeah, it's got to go back on the wall.' And then he was like, 'There's a metal box in that garage. Did he smoke?' And she said no. Then when she got home, she texted me saying, 'Oh my god, I'm freaked out.' She'd told her mum about the metal box thing. She said it was her dad's cigarette box in the garage.

So that's how intuitive he is, but like I said, he's especially in touch with my feelings. I can't get away with anything.

I used to just think Tommy was hard work to deal with. He was hard work to live with. But then when I had Brody, I changed. I think when you're desperate to make something work and you fight for your relationship, or fight for your family, you look closer and you look more in-depth. You really have to. It's not as easy to just walk away when you've got a baby. I needed an answer because I'd seen a change in Tommy. He didn't have a lot of patience. It wasn't because of Brody, but around that time, all of life got more stressful.

His company got bigger, we moved house, had a baby. I think when you're a parent, when you've got a child, you have to be on the same page with certain things when it comes to your child. Before, if I had said that sock was black but he said it was blue, it wouldn't really matter. But when you've got a child, you have to think the same in certain situations. We realised that we both felt differently and needed to work out how to get back on the same page again. Brody made us fight for us where we probably wouldn't have before.

I think the fear of losing me and Brody made Tommy go for the ADHD assessment. Why else would he have done it? He'd got through, what, thirty years? No one had ever picked it up. School didn't; not even his parents. The school always thought it was something like dyslexia, and his parents never challenged it because back then, no one did. Schools just marked him down as the naughty kid.

He felt relieved when he got the diagnosis. He actually felt like he was being listened to. We spoke one day and he asked me things he's never asked before.

'You know your brain?'

'Yeah?'

'Have you got music playing in your head all the time?'

'Um, no.'

'What? In my brain right now, I've got someone talking. Then there's music, and I'm thinking about something different too.'

I thought, *That sounds exhausting.* When he explained what his brain actually does, what it sounds like, I started to understand what he was going through. We'd never had that chat before. So when he had help and then got on medication, he said, 'Wow, this is the first time I've ever been able to think clearly. It's silent. It's weird.'

Thinking about what he was experiencing, with all those different sounds in his head, it makes sense that when the baby screamed or the dog barked, it would trigger him because he couldn't handle the extra noise.

We've been doing more research because ADHD's hereditary, so Brody might also have it. I went to a charity event recently and a woman there said she didn't get diagnosed until later in life. Because she was a girl, and she wasn't disruptive but her mind would wander off, the teachers would have a go at her and call her naughty. The same thing happened to Tommy: he was disruptive because he couldn't understand what they were saying, or he'd be bored and couldn't concentrate and they'd tell him he was naughty, and remove him from the class.

We really need to change the conversation around ADHD and mental health in general. It starts with making talking about it less taboo, making people feel like they can open up about how they're feeling and what they're going through. Then we need to make sure all the people who need extra help, like with medication, get it, as well as being offered talking therapies and coping strategies.

Remember . . .

If you're struggling with your mental health, or feel you're not being seen or understood, go to your GP and ask for a referral. It's so important to get the help you need. You deserve it.

♡

'I really needed to
take care of myself.
You can't ignore things'

♡

I wish I knew ...

How to find myself
after becoming a mum

I felt lost after becoming a mum.

It was partly because my body looked so different. I looked like a different person. Then I also had this person to keep alive and that's a mad thing to comprehend.

At first, everyone was round at my house, which I liked. But then normal life resumed – Tommy went back to work, the nans went home – and I thought, *What am I supposed to do now?* I was thinking, *Er, what's my job again? What am I doing? Is this my job now, motherhood?* And I realised that, well, yeah – it was. It was such an odd transition to go through. Suddenly, every day mirrored the last.

I didn't know how to dress any more. Who was I? I didn't know what would suit my new body, what I should be wearing. I was saying, 'Do I have to wear different things, now I'm a mum?' Those first few months were wild. Everyone piling in, helping out. Tommy was home for a short while and we were all in a bubble. I had become a mum for the first time, Tommy had become a dad, the nans had become nans. It was a lot of firsts and we were in it together. But then they all left, and a life of looking after Brody was ongoing, and you've got to figure it out yourself. I was just a bit lost, thinking, *Well, what do I do every day now? I dunno what to do.* Leaving the house for the first time was scary. Getting in the car for the first time: scary. Just getting out is scary when you're a new mum, isn't it?

I was shocked that everyone had to go back to normal life and go back to work. It seemed like they all knew what they were meant to be doing but me. I was just lost in new motherhood. And I didn't know what to do work-wise either. My agent would be saying, 'Right, when are you going back to work?' And I'd respond, 'Well, what do I even wanna do?' Because all my time pre-Brody was focused on having this baby and going at a hundred miles per hour. And then when I had him, I thought, *What now? What space am I in?* I remember getting some jobs promoting mother and baby products, and I didn't even know how to use the products yet myself. It was all new to me. I didn't even know how to use a bouncer. I mean, now I'm an actual professional, I could do it with my eyes closed. But at the time everything was just scary. And I found it really, really hard. I think dressing myself was so weird because I wanted to wear baggy clothes (and I kind of still do; I'm still in that era). I think it's a comfort thing. The thought of putting on a tight dress just freaks me out. But pre-Brody, that's all I'd wear.

I went back to work straight away after having Brody. I had no time off at all. I started filming my show four days after I had him. Some people say getting back to work helps in terms of your identity and feeling like yourself again, but I didn't feel that. It all felt a lot harder because now I was trying to do the same work but with a baby with me all the time. In some ways, getting back to filming so quickly did help me feel as if I was back in the real world again, doing a job I did know how to do, but it was really overwhelming, too.

You do lose yourself when you have a kid, because you become their mum first. Now, I'm Brody's mum, but I have to keep reminding myself that I'm Georgia as well. The me before him hasn't gone anywhere, it's just a transition into a new phase. And that's OK.

I used to have so much more confidence before I had Brody, which is odd because I've achieved so much more and feel like I'm a much better person since I've had him. But in some ways, I knew myself better then. Now, I don't really know myself as much. It will take time to figure out who I am as well as being mum to Brody.

You change in so many ways after becoming a mum. It changes your body, your career, your relationship, your friendships, your holidays even! But, underneath all that, you're still *you*. And in time, you'll see that all the changes are what makes it amazing. It's worth it.

'I felt lost after becoming a mum'

How to find yourself after becoming a mum:

When you become a mum, it's like a whole new identity, which can feel amazing but it can also throw you a little bit. Here are some questions to ask yourself if you're feeling a bit lost . . .

- *What did I like most about myself before having a baby?*

- *What did I like the least about myself back then?*

- *In what amazing ways have I changed since having a baby?*

- *What can I do now that I couldn't do before?*

- *What's the best thing about becoming a mum?*

I wish I knew ...

What it would be like becoming a mum-fluencer

On social media, in the parenting/mum space, people are everywhere, with opinions here, opinions there. There's so much conflicting information online, as well as on social media, and it can be overwhelming.

When I have my second baby, I know exactly what I want. I know exactly what products I'll want to use. You have to try out everything, don't you? Everyone will try telling you what's best but you're the only person making the decision.

I was overwhelmed by how much I needed to buy for a baby. How could this tiny, tiny human need all of these things? I felt like my brain had opened up to reveal another space: mum brain space. Its only role was thinking about what I needed for Brody every day. It's crazy, isn't it? You don't realise how much you go through in your head when you become a mum.

Before, I'd just think about myself all day. What do I fancy eating? What do I want to do tonight? But now, by 9 a.m., I've already done so much work. Just getting yourself and your baby ready – dressed, fed – takes a lot of effort and organising. I've got to think about Brody and all his needs while still thinking about my work, friends, family.

The online community saved me, though. They made me feel less alone. I'd put a question up on my Instagram grid and they'd answer it, giving me loads of tips. I'd give them tips back, if I ever had any. It quickly started to feel like we were all part of this same community. It's like a lifeline for new mums, because if I didn't have Instagram, who would I ask? My mum had me years ago and things are different now.

The Instagram mum community is a quick and easy way to connect with loads of mums. A lot of the time it's me asking the questions and people helping me out. I'm not embarrassed to be vulnerable and say that I don't know everything. But then sometimes, I'll share a tip or a product that I knew will help out other mums, so it feels reciprocal in that way. I'm so much happier being in this mum space where it feels like there's so much more support and solidarity.

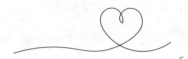

Don't be scared to:

1. *Don't be scared to show your postnatal body.*

2. *Don't be scared to ask for help.*

3. *Don't be scared to say how you feel.*

4. *Don't be scared to be honest.*

5. *Don't be scared to show the hard bits.*

♡

'I felt like my
brain opened up to
reveal another space:
mum brain space!'

♡

I wish I knew ...

Where to get mum tips

I found so many people to help me when I was trying to work out what I needed for Brody as a baby. I didn't know who knew best, so I just reached out to ask my questions. I knew a woman who had a baby shop, and she's known for telling you exactly what you need. I also found Victoria, who I absolutely adore and who works as a sleep coach. I still talk to her a lot. My midwife, Pat, was great; I asked her a lot of questions. My mum and Bev were fantastic too. And then when we got to the weaning stage, I found a woman on Instagram who was amazing. I was worried about weaning Brody and she gave me loads of tips.

It's all about finding people who can support you. It's hard, though, and a bit scary because there's so much different information out there. You'll get one person saying you can't give water to babies, while someone else is saying you have to give them water. And then my mum will say, 'Well, in my day . . .' And then there's the decision about whether you're going to breastfeed or bottle-feed. Also, whether you're going to co-sleep or have your baby in their own cot. Everyone's got their own ideas, so you have to go with what you think is right. I was sure I wanted to bottle-feed and I knew Brody would be sleeping in his own cot, rather than with me. I didn't take anyone's advice on this, I just went with my gut.

I found the people I could trust, but then sometimes, you've just got to go with your gut. It's scary, but you have to. At the end of the day, you are the mum. You are your baby's mum and you know best, even if it feels like you don't. You do.

My good friend Amy and I had our babies ten days apart, which was so nice, because I had someone there going through it the whole time. If Brody wasn't sleeping, I'd be like, 'Oh my god, are you going through this?' And she'd say, 'Yep, me too.' I was lucky because it seemed both our babies were literally going through all the same things at the same time. Whether it was sleep regression or teething, we were then in it together. And it was perfect.

'I just went with my gut'

Find your trusty mum advisors:

- *Find people in your local area having a baby at a similar time, so you can go through it together and help answer each other's questions.*

- *Online friends can be amazing for sharing tips with, too. Are you a member of any new mum groups?*

- *If you have a specific need – like your baby isn't sleeping well – turn to the professionals. Get proper support from professionals when you need it. That's what they are there for.*

- *Ask your own mum, aunties, sisters and friends for advice. But take it with a pinch of salt. If you don't like their answer, don't take the advice. And know that it's OK to do that!*

I wish I knew ...
Time with friends is so important

If you have a support network around you, or if someone you trust has offered to take care of your baby, take them up on it!

I'd really recommend going out for little trips with your friends, and if you can't manage a whole day, just take a few hours. When I was struggling in the early months, my mum would say, 'Just go out and get some lunch with your mates, or go and have a bit of breakfast by yourself' – little things that get you out of the house. Even just getting in the car and going for a drive to McDonald's – it's reclaiming little bits that you used to do.

It reminds you of who you are and it gives you

some time with your friends, or by yourself, to feel like you again. It's like therapy, isn't it? And we all know we need it. Take one evening or a few daytime hours with your friends – those seemingly 'little' chats are so important.

After the first couple of months with Brody, I thought, *I'm done. I'm ready to go out and have some fun with my friends.* I remember running out the door at that point! I didn't want to leave him for those first months, but there does come a time when you need to get back moments for yourself. You're not just Mum. You're you.

At first, when the nans suggested helping with night feeds, I said no. Then one day, when I was crying because I was so tired, I started letting them take over and do little bits. It was the same with going out; I felt like I was all right to leave him at home with them for a few hours. I got a glimpse of what life was like outside the baby bubble and thought, *This is lovely, let's do it again soon.*

When you've managed to get out of the house for an hour or two, you come back more refreshed and you're ready to start again. Motherhood is a twenty-four-hour job. It's always a part of you, even when you're away from your child. So you're not abandoning your baby when you take a few moments for yourself. The first three months especially are a lot. There's no release. So hanging out with your friends brings you back to yourself and gives you a chance to breathe. I felt like I was a better mum if I'd had a night's sleep or a few hours out. If you've got the support to do that, you're as lucky as I was.

My top tips for strengthening your friendships:

1. *Make time for each other. I see my friends as much as possible.*

2. *Know that friendships come and go, and that's OK.*

3. *But hold on dearly to the friends who are always there.*

4. *Be open, honest and real with your friends, and expect the same in reverse.*

5. *When things feel difficult, try to talk it out. You don't always know what the other person is going through.*

♡

'Motherhood is
a twenty-four-hour job.
It's always a part of you,
even when you're away
from your child'

♡

I wish I knew ...

How much you need your partner's support after birth

Tommy and I are a good team. But having a baby is always going to introduce a different dynamic into a relationship, as you build your family together. At first, we both struggled to find a new normal, and then I think we started getting into a good routine. I'd do the night feeds and he would do the morning. It was good, once we got into that rhythm.

I think Tommy struggled with the newness in the house at the beginning. Life as we knew it had changed and although he was asleep at night, he could still hear the baby. I guess he probably struggled with me being the way I was too. He didn't say that, but our roles changed. I'm the organised person in the house and I always sort things out, so I can imagine he probably struggled with the fact that I wasn't that person for a while. He had to step up even more.

I spoke to him about how I felt I'd lost my identity a bit. When my mental health got worse, and he spoke up for me and announced I wasn't right to our mums and the midwife, he knew I was finding it hard.

Soon after that, there was one day that I will always remember. I got upset and said I didn't know how to dress with my new body. I was getting really frustrated and I didn't want to go out anywhere because I didn't know what to wear any more. Tommy decided we would have a shopping day, and he took me shopping and allowed me to dress like me again. I got nice leggings and little jumpers – basically smarter versions of what I'd been wearing, because until then, I'd been in my oversized, old, baggy pregnancy stuff.

He started getting me out more, and I realised,

Oh yeah, I like clothes, that's something I used to enjoy and something I can do again. It's not gone. He was so sweet, helping me choose bits out, saying, 'That would look nice. You like leggings, try them on, and get that little jumper.'

He saw what I needed – not new clothes, but a new way of thinking about myself. I needed that pick-me-up as a reminder.

Remember . . .

Dads find the transition to becoming parents hard too. It's different for them – they don't physically have a part to play in the pregnancy and birth – but they still experience changes. So keep the communication open, tell them how you're feeling, ask how they're feeling and make sure you do nice things for each other.

♡

'Having a baby is
always going to introduce
a different dynamic into a
relationship, as you build
your family together'

♡

I wish I knew ...

That I would be a different person after having children

I've become a different person since having Brody, because Georgia-before-Brody didn't know what I know now. She had different priorities, and had nothing really to think about, except for the dog. I can still be both Mum Georgia and Georgia-who-works, as long as I have good childcare!

Before Brody, I was up for doing all the jobs. Even when I was pregnant, I was on it. I wanted, and still want, to be financially secure, to have my own income. But now, my agent will be messaging me saying, 'You need to do this; you've got a shoot day next week, there's prep to do.' And in my head,

I'm thinking, *I can't take it on. My brain's too full.* Sometimes Brody just wants me to hold him all day and won't let me put him down. I do then just blank everyone's messages. He always comes first.

By the time Brody goes to bed, I'm absolutely drained, mentally and physically. I catch Tommy for an hour to go over plans and life in general, and then I'm knackered and I don't want to talk to anyone else. I don't even want to think, I just want to sit in silence.

It will be so much easier when Brody goes to nursery. I'll have my set days that I won't have Brody there, saying, 'Mum, Mum.' When he's doing that, I'm instantly distracted and forget whatever I'm meant to be doing. Then I start cooking lunch, tidying up, sorting the dog's dinner. And whatever that message someone just sent said completely disappears from my consciousness, like it never even happened. Sometimes I open messages and won't reply for three weeks.

I've considered whether I should be a full-time mum and give up work entirely but I do love what

I do. I like earning my own money. I don't think I could just rely on Tommy because it would stress me out – and because I'm wired to want to earn my own money. I think that comes from my mum and dad splitting up, because Mum never earned her own money. I remember her saying to me, 'Make sure you always have your own money, just in case.' Things change, and then you've got no control.

When my mum and dad separated, my mum stayed at my friend's house. I got a job doing an advert and received a big lump of money for it. I'd never had that before. When I got it, I gave some of it to my mum to rent a house for six months. I was so proud of myself. I got my mum and my siblings into a rented house. Mum just needed that lump sum to do it. She paid me back after, but it meant so much to me to be able to help out.

Then something really rubbish happened and people started mocking the advert I did online, doing piss-takes and putting on a voice. I kept getting tagged in the comments on social media and it was awful. But they didn't know my story.

They didn't know that I was working to help my mum and siblings start a new chapter in their lives. And I'd do it ten times over for them.

'Georgia-before-Brody didn't know what I know now'

Remember . . .

- *In some ways, you'll feel like a different person after having a baby. And that's OK. It's OK to change.*

- *But the old you is still tucked in there, too.*

- *If you have the choice between being a full-time mum and returning to work, do what feels right for you and your family. There is no one way that suits everyone.*

- *You do you.*

I wish I knew ...

You have to pick your battles

Brody is only two but he rules my life. Tommy and I always laugh and say, 'How can a two-year-old just take over a house?' We both feel like Brody has all the power but we do have to remind ourselves that we are the adults. And I have to remind Brody that too, sometimes. He's a very funny little boy.

Obviously, as the adults in the situation, we always have the final say, but there's an element of compromise involved when you're parenting a two-year-old. You have to choose your battles.

Some days, if I'm a bit tired, I might let him get away with a bit more. I'll say, 'Oh, go on then, have another chocolate.'

I never judge another mum because you don't know what that mum's been through that morning, or how they are choosing to parent their child. Let's say there's a kid lying on the ground, refusing to move, and so she walks off. By that point, getting to the park, she's probably had five rows with that kid and she no doubt thinks, *Just do what the fuck you want then.* Let them lie on the floor refusing to move. And then she walks off, knowing he'll probably get up and follow her. I get that completely. We've all been there.

That's why I say choose your battles. If they want to wear two different-coloured wellies, let them. Or five different outfits one on top of the other – who cares? They want to wear their pyjamas, does it really matter? We all have those days.

Our morning routine goes something like this:

First thing in the morning, I take Brody downstairs and I make him a bottle. I don't even go for a wee until I've done that. Then I do a wee, make a tea and I sit on the sofa with Brody. He has his bottle, I have my tea and we just take five minutes. After we've chilled for a bit, he'll start playing. Then I'll start making his breakfast. I make myself a shake. I take Brody upstairs with me and I've started bathing him in the mornings, so he'll bathe while I shower. I brush his teeth and get him ready. It's a big operation, though. I'm dealing with a two-year-old here, so he doesn't want to do much. Everything's a negotiation and it sometimes turns into a bit of a row. Sometimes I have to force him to do things, like get dressed. I have to take his babygro off myself and say, 'Come on now, Brody, we need to take it off because it's really dirty.' He's got a bit of an obsessive personality. He'll say he doesn't want to put his babygro on at night and then in the morning, he doesn't want to take it off. I have to tell him that there are loads of tiny ant poos in there and he's going to step on them if he doesn't take it off. That usually does the trick.

Sometimes, doing his teeth is such a battle, I don't do it. I try, but sometimes I can't deal with that battle. I need to change his toothpaste because he's going through a stage of not wanting minty toothpaste. I bought a strawberry one so I'm going to try that now. I made the mistake of giving him mint toothpaste when he was a baby and now it's like it's scarred him for life. The things we have to think about, eh?

Choose your battles

- *Some things are essential so you have to be patient . . . or trick them into doing them.*

- *Some things aren't – remind yourselves which ones. In which case, drop them and move on with your day.*

♡

'There's an element of compromise involved when you're parenting a two-year-old . . .'

♡

I wish I knew ...

How hard motherhood would be

Everything's hard, especially at the beginning.

But I wish that people had told me more about how it was going to actually be, and then maybe I wouldn't have beaten myself up about it when I found it hard. If I'd have known about all the things that people struggle with, I would have embraced it all more, rather than thinking, *Why am I struggling so much? Why do I find it so hard?* I thought I just wasn't good enough.

Second time round, I'll know it's going to be tough. But I'll also know it's just a series of phases, and that everyone finds it hard – it's just that people don't tell you. They only talk about the good bits, about how cute their baby is, because they think that's what they're meant to do. That people won't think they are a good mum if they struggle with anything.

People are starting to be more open about what they find hard with motherhood. When I had Brody, it felt like no one spoke about how you change, or how long it can take to connect with the baby. I never heard any of that. I never saw it anywhere – on TV, online.

I think people are embarrassed to admit they're struggling. There's nothing to be embarrassed about, though, because if more people admitted it, then you wouldn't feel alone. That was the problem. I felt alone because I thought everyone else had gone with it, embraced it and was dealing with new motherhood like it was a breeze. It was like every other new mum had this natural instinct, everyone else was a natural at it, except me. So then I started believing I wasn't a natural, and maybe I should have just stuck to being a dog mum. I really struggled, and when I started talking about it with all my friends, they would all say, 'Oh yeah, I had that.' And I thought, *I wish you'd said that earlier.* I'd been giving myself such a hard time!

Hearing the hard stuff before having a baby wouldn't have stopped me having Brody because he wasn't planned anyway. But what it would've done was make me more vocal early on. I'd have admitted that I was really struggling with his sleep and my lack of it. That I was struggling with how to put on a nappy and make a bottle. I'd have said I was struggling with people trying to tell me to breastfeed. I'd have felt better, but instead I kept it all inside because I was embarrassed. I thought it was just me.

If I'd known what it was going to be like, it would all have become a lot less scary. I like to know what's coming, because I'm a control freak. I like to prepare. I don't like shocks or surprises and motherhood was all a complete shock and surprise, and I had no control over it whatsoever.

I never watched *One Born Every Minute* to prepare myself. I didn't need to watch that to prepare for giving birth because, deep down, I knew I wasn't going to give birth that way. I knew I wasn't going to have a vaginal birth. I ended up having a planned C-section because Brody was breech. I sensed that he was going to be breech before it happened. I'd been doing all of these courses to prepare myself and I didn't feel scared. I'd moved from spending my whole life feeling panicked about the idea of giving birth to feeling OK about it. And I thought, *Why am I feeling so calm now?* when deep down, giving birth was the worst thing I could possibly imagine. I realised it was because I knew I wouldn't be doing it. The doctors said he was breech in January, and I had until May to give birth, so he might turn around, but I knew he wouldn't.

It was scary, the thought of being completely cut open, and the risks that come with it. But I think what scared me the most about the idea of a vaginal birth was not knowing when the baby was going to come. It freaked me out. The idea of waiting for it; waiting for the waters to break so you could meet your baby would be a complete surprise.

Next time, I will opt for a C-section again as my experience was good. I know that Brody will be taken care of and I can make sure he's sorted.

I'm hoping my next baby will be a girl. We need more female energy in the house, to balance out Tommy, Brody and the dog. We need another girl in the mix.

Remember . . .

If you're finding new motherhood hard, you're not alone. Everyone struggles, in their own way, it's just that some are more vocal than others. Some people keep the hard bits secret, as they feel ashamed. Fuck that. Be open and honest with people you can trust, and watch how the support rolls right on in.

'I thought
I just wasn't
good enough'

I wish I knew ...
You don't have to breastfeed

I didn't exactly feel pressured to breastfeed, but everyone around me kept asking about it. I mostly ignored them. When I visited my midwives, they'd all be saying, 'So, are you going to breastfeed?' In my head, I was saying, *No way*, but to them, because they kept asking, I'd sometimes say, 'Oh yeah, I'll give it a try.'

When I went to the hospital where I was going to have Brody, I met my midwife, Pat, who went on to deliver him. I love her, I still talk to her now. She said to me, 'Are you going to breastfeed?' And I said, 'I'm not sure.' She said, 'Georgia, if you're saying you don't know, you're probably not going to do it so take the pressure off yourself and just say you're not going to. It's OK.' She's amazing. So from then on, I said, 'No, I'm not going to.'

I never had an urge to breastfeed. I needed Pat to tell me that it was OK if I didn't. I'm such a big advocate of doing whatever works for you. If you don't want to breastfeed, fine. If you do, fine. I'm fully open online and when anyone asks my opinion, I say, 'It's my body, it's my baby, I know best.' If my baby's fed and watered and he's loved, then he's fine. Absolutely fine. I always say to people, 'There's a hundred people in the room – you'll never, ever, be able to spot who was breastfed and who wasn't. So who cares?'

It seems like such a big deal at the time. But really, who gives a shit? If you don't want to do it and it's not right for your family, that is more important than being forced into it. It especially wouldn't have worked with my family and home dynamic, but that doesn't even matter. If you don't want to breastfeed, you don't have to, and that's it.

Tommy was also taking Brody off in the mornings from 5 a.m. and giving him a bottle, and he wouldn't have been able to do that unless I pumped, and pumping wouldn't have worked for me. It felt like so much more pressure and I had so much pressure on me already. I was in a really bad place, so adding breastfeeding into the mix, having to be alone with Brody every time I breastfed, would've really sent me over the edge, I think.

I knew what was right for my family: bottle-feeding. Also, Brody was a big baby, and he was starving. He was eight pounds nine ounces – and he was ten days early. They said that I could have had a ten-pound baby, because those last three weeks are just about gaining extra fat.

It's funny, because it wasn't just the midwives laying on the pressure about breastfeeding, it's everywhere online too. On Instagram, I'd get mums sending out the message that 'breast is best' and I'd always respond by saying 'fed is best'. I have friends who breastfed and loved it – it's all good. As long as you're happy and your baby's happy, that's the most important thing. I think because I'm very straight on the subject – I'm very black and white about it –

people don't come for me on Instagram! They don't start on me. It's when you're on the fence, wondering if you might like to give breastfeeding a try, that's when you end up getting bombarded by opinions.

I was very certain on not wanting to breastfeed but there were other things that I wasn't so sure about, things like sterilising bottles, or knowing whether or not I should swaddle. I questioned myself the whole time. I wondered if I should be getting into more of a routine with naps and mornings.

Looking back now, I actually think I did a really good job. I just couldn't see it at the time. It sounds like I was quite decisive but I was phoning my mum, panicking, saying, 'Is this the right thing to do?' My mum's a very calming person, which helped.

But motherhood was all so new to me, and there were so many considerations. I probably knew deep down inside what I wanted to do and then panicked on the surface, and had to check with other people who were already mums.

I had all the right people around me, so I was lucky that they helped to confirm what I already knew.

Remember . . .

If you want to breastfeed, great. If you want to bottle-feed, great. Fed is best. Do what's right for you, your baby and your little family.

♡

'If you don't want to,
you don't have to,
and that's it'

♡

I wish I knew ...

To take one step at a time

Everything's a phase, so don't stress about it.

When you have a newborn, and you're worrying about sleep patterns and getting them into routines, you don't realise that this is a phase that will end one day. But it will. So take one step at a time. Just think about what's going on that day; how to get your baby sleeping that night. Try not to think about everything that's coming after that.

There's a saying that you should worry about the step, not the staircase, and I think that's so true. I'd get myself in a panic when Brody was a baby, thinking if I did this certain thing, it would mean he might never get into a good routine. But you've got to keep reminding yourself that it's all a phase, it will pass, everything will be OK. Worry about now, not next month, because next month, it'll be something different.

If your baby wants a dummy, give them a dummy and deal with how you're going to wean them off when that time comes. Go with it for now if it's working, and think about the next steps when it's time to move on.

There will always be mums who have different opinions to you. Some of them will be very opinionated and pushy. You get all different sorts of mums and parents. You get what I call the earth mums, very organic in every way and who believe breast is best. They're sometimes a bit too opinionated, I think. And then you get mums who are very chilled, just get the boob out whenever, go with the flow, no routine at all. I like those mums. I'm the complete opposite, though. I remember this influencer on Instagram saying co-sleeping's the best for them, but I needed my room and my bed as a place firmly for me. I like my own time. It may be selfish, but I love a routine. Obviously, in the newborn stage, I didn't have one, but when Brody was a bit older and the right age for a routine, I got professional help and I stuck to what they told me. I was strict. People know not to turn up at my house around Brody's nap times too!

Having a routine has meant that when he's gone to bed at 7 p.m., I've got my evenings. There are loads of different types of mums because there's loads of different ways to be a parent. Everyone does things differently, but it's important just to find what works for you and your family.

Remember . . .

- *One step at a time.*

- *Don't think too far ahead.*

- *If you live in the future, you'll miss the present.*

- *Worry about the step, not the staircase.*

♡

'Everything's a phase,
so don't stress about it'

♡

I wish I knew ...

What would happen if I joined a reality show

TOWIE happened so quickly for me that I had no time to think about it. There was no assessment of whether it was the right thing to do for me, I just dived straight in. Over the years, I sometimes wondered what it would have been like if I'd kept my shop. What would I be doing now?

I was totally focused on being on the show and doing a good job of it, so I had spent no time thinking about alternative paths.

Right from the start, *TOWIE* felt completely right. It happened out of the blue, and I went with it. Although I'm a control freak, I was able to go with the flow on that show. I loved the freedom of it. We had to grow up fast because we were dealing with a lot. But we also got to *really* enjoy our twenties, being out filming with our friends every day. We'd go on trips and to fun events. It was the best thing ever. They were the best days of my life. Before Brody, obviously.

We were contained in the show, so we weren't completely free, but we didn't have to worry too much about life outside of it. I think that's where the sense of freedom came from. We'd go to bed, wake up and go on these trips. We'd be filmed all the time but could drink and eat good food, chat all day – and get paid for it. We literally got paid to be young and free.

Meanwhile, other people were getting up at 5 a.m., getting on trains and going into cities to work a full day. We were working a few hours and having the best time.

Being on the show creates a bond that you will never experience unless you're in it. That bond is still there; there's a respect that we'll never lose.

And I love that TOWIE is still on because it reminds me of that time in my life. If it ever finished, I'd be so sad. I wouldn't have left if I hadn't had a baby. *Baby Steps*, our show now, is completely different. It feels like a different life.

I missed out on a lot of family and friend stuff during those years. Things like baby showers, birthdays and holidays. I was never able to commit because I never knew when my day off would be. When all my girls were meeting up, they'd invite me, but I could hardly ever go. I was disconnected from the outside world because I was filming six days a week and so I never knew if I could be there for them. It was quite frustrating for them; for anyone on the outside. That's why you become friends with people who are in the same industry, because they get it.

I'm still friends with all the TOWIE lot. I don't see them loads, maybe once a month, but we've still got WhatsApp groups that we chat on. Lydia and Amber are really good friends of mine; they're two of my best friends, so I don't have to see them all the time because we're so close anyway. When I do see them, it's like no time has passed at all.

We're just like a little family. A weird little family, with a proper bond. It was TOWIE that gave us all the lives we have now. I did it for a long time, though. I started when I was twenty-two and did it for seven years. That's a long time to be in a job. Especially one where you're working so many unpredictable hours.

There were times I found it hard being in the public eye, like when I got my nose job and there were so many people criticising me for doing so. I also found it hard when there were conflicts on the show. You'd get into an argument and then you'd have everyone's opinions on what had happened. When it got really tough for me, I'd have to turn my phone off and say to Tommy, 'Take me away, take me somewhere else, please.' We'd go for a weekend away because I just couldn't face the online criticism. We had no control over it. We were watching the TOWIE episodes when the public watched them, so we never knew what was going to be shown.

We'd have to watch every episode so that we knew what was going on in the show, because in the next episode, you'd have to refer to the last episode and whatever had made the edit. It was savage. You'd hear people slagging you off, and you'd have to sit through that. And then it would hit social media, and you'd have to deal with it a second time.

Back then, the audience was young. You'd get trolled a lot. But, thankfully, now I'm in such a different space, my audience and the people I'm talking to are mostly fellow mums and I love them.

All my family watched me on TOWIE. My nan and all my cousins in Ireland, everyone. Everyone loved it. They found it hard if I'd been in some kind of conflict, or a row, of course. Some of my friends watched it too and they weren't jealous that I was on the show but sometimes, I felt that they didn't understand, and I get it. I wouldn't have understood either. I think they got used to it as the years went on.

I missed one of my friend's hen dos because I was away filming. When we were away, we never knew how long we'd be there for. Halfway through, they'd say, 'Right, some cast are going home and some are staying.' It would depend on the storyline.

I know all my friends got upset about me not being able to come because of the show, but at the time, that was how I earned my money. And when you're filming, you film for a period of time and then you're off for eight weeks or so. In those eight weeks, I didn't earn any money.

I did feel guilty but they understood and we ended up doing an extra hen do that I could come to.

I used to put TOWIE first because that was my job. People didn't always get it because it's not an office job, so they didn't take it, or me, too seriously.

I had so much fun on the show. I would not change a thing. I always say that with the good times, there are sad times too, and it helps you to grow as a person. I have no regrets. And I'll watch TOWIE forever.

Remember . . .

Prioritise whatever you need to prioritise to get through. That might be work and earning money, it might be raising your child, or it might be something else. But if you can't attend an event because of your job or baby, so be it. Your real friends will understand (even if they're a bit disappointed, and that's OK too).

♡

'We're just like
a little family.
A weird little
family . . .'

♡

I wish I knew ...

What social media would really be like

When I started TOWIE a decade ago, I wasn't on social media. Instagram had just been launched, so then everyone started getting it. I remember getting a few thousand followers and being so excited. Back in those days, every time someone messaged me, I'd message them back. We'd have chats. I can't do that now sadly, but I still love seeing people's messages come in.

If I was in a bad scene on TOWIE, like if I was having a row with someone, or in a sensitive scene, or doing anything that wasn't the ordinary, I'd know that when I went on social media, I'd get backlash for it. People would private message and comment on my pictures and videos. What's especially hard is that you film the scene and you're going through that argument in real time, then you watch the show and experience it for a second time, then you go on social media and get trolled or inundated with comments and opinions on what you did wrong.

I'd never avoid going on social media. People say, 'Well, just don't look.' But it's much more easily said than done because you're intrigued about what the response will be to your show. You want to read it but you also know you're going to get so much shit. People slag you off and abuse you no matter what. They say you're disgusting, ask how you could have said a certain thing. People take what they see on telly very seriously and get very dramatic about it.

In some of the rows on *TOWIE*, there would be a divide created – your fans versus the other person's fans. They'd start rowing among themselves in the comments. I learnt very quickly that those arguments were fickle! It's all down to the edit and whether it goes in your favour. That's why you have to just be yourself on shows like that. If you try to hide anything, viewers see right through it.

Obviously, the show edited and put out what they thought were two sides but sometimes, they could have missed a vital point of a row and I'd be on the phone to producers, having a go. I did that a lot, actually. They'd apologise and say, 'Well, in your next scene, just say that bit that we cut out.' There's not much they can do. Once it's out, it's out. That's when I would struggle most – when I knew that I was in the right and it looked like I was in the wrong. Then I'd get trouble online for something that I had no control over.

Sometimes, I'd be more guarded in scenes so as not to get trolled, but the problem with me is I can't act and I just come out with things. I used to sign out of Instagram for a bit and get off my phone and then pray it'd all be finished by the time I logged back on. But I couldn't just delete Instagram because that was part of my work; I got paid for certain posts. It can be the best thing and the worst thing at the same time.

I received a lot of abuse when I had my nose done. There were loads of mean comments with people calling me Michael Jackson for about a year. 'What's she done to her face?' they would ask. Lots of viewers can't handle you changing over time either. I started on the show when I was twenty-two, and I left at thirty. My fashion had changed, my looks had changed, I wore different make-up, changed up my hair. I'd evolved. But the viewers seemed to forget that they do that as well! They would point out how much I had changed and I'd think, *Well, I'm glad I look different now, compared to how I did when I was twenty-two.*

It always hurt when people commented on how I looked. But eventually, I kind of got used to it. If someone said I was ugly, I just thought, *OK, thanks, I don't give a shit what you think.* Now, my worst comment to see would be if someone said something about me as Brody's mum. That's when I'd see red.

Everyone always says how happy Brody is on our show, or online, and I don't get slated for that. That being said, the other day, Tommy put Brody in the car seat and people were saying, 'He's too big for that car seat.' We were like, 'Well, he's not because the car seat says it's for up to four years of age and he's two.' I think it was the angle he was sitting at that meant he just looked bigger in it than he is. He's a big boy. There's always someone who's going to be saying something but you've got to just know how good you are as a mum and not let it bother you.

Whatever I post, there will always be loads of nice comments and then some that are a bit annoying. Like when I recently posted about how Brody will be starting nursery soon and I've been feeling a bit worried, loads of people said, 'Oh, it will be fine, don't worry.' But then others were saying, 'Well, just don't send him, then.' Stupid, annoying comments like that. I was saying, 'Well, I'm going to feel like this when he goes to school but I legally have to send him at a certain point and yeah, I don't legally have to send him to nursery but it's going to be good for him.' I'm not bothered about those people, they can just bore off.

One of the worst things about the TOWIE days, in terms of social media, was that people would be telling me I was fat, or that I'd gained weight. They'd often say, 'You're pregnant! You're pregnant!' And I'd lose loads of weight and they'd all say, 'You're too skinny.' So you couldn't ever win. You get trolls telling you your nose is big but then you have a nose job and get them telling you you're Michael Jackson. I block a lot of people. I remember looking at my block list and laughing because I had so many people on there. What's weird is I'd get some women trolling me, the same ones all the time, and I'd look at their profiles and they'd have kids. I'd think, *You're trolling me, but you're a mum, and you've got kids my age?* I used to reply sometimes and say, 'I'd be so embarrassed if you were my mum.' I learnt not to rise to it over time, but sometimes I couldn't help it.

The trolls like it if I reply. But I would sometimes be getting properly trolled and I'd reply and they'd say, 'I'm so sorry, I love you.' And I'd be thinking, *You're a proper weirdo. You've just trolled me for months and now I've replied, telling you to shut up, you're saying you're sorry and you love me?* Some of these people are nuts. Over the years, there have been some absolute nutters.

Now I love it because I've got really loyal followers within the motherhood community. If I'm feeling really shitty, and I put a post up, I know mums will be coming to me, sending me messages and making me feel normal again. I'm in my own lane, and in my own space now.

I don't set any limits or boundaries in terms of how much time I spend online, or on Instagram. Obviously when you've got a baby, you're not on it all day, are you?

I never check the likes or engagement on my personal posts, but I do for the work ones because the better they do, the more work I get. Though I'm always interested to see what resonates with my audience. I probably should have a proper strategy for it. I just post what I think at the time! Intuitive posting. That works better for me.

That's why I wouldn't want my daughter going

on reality TV, though. I had the best time but it's changed. I just feel like social media's different now and you've got to be really strong-minded to do it. I'd be scared for her.

I've never been stalked since TOWIE, but when I was younger, about thirteen, I was in a beauty competition called Miss Teen Queen and I got to the final. Back in those days, people could get hold of your phone number and address so easily, from the Yellow Pages or similar, and this man started calling my house and asking for me. The first time, I wasn't there and my mum thought it must have been a teacher so she said, 'Oh, Georgia's not here at the moment.' But then he knew I lived there and he called back and my sister answered, so she handed me the phone. His voice was really weird and he said, 'Hello, Georgia, was that your sister on the phone?' I thought, *What the fuck?* He then started telling me all the sexual things he was going to do to me.

I was only young and I completely freaked out. I slammed the phone down. I was really scared and he kept calling back. When my mum answered, he put the phone down. Eventually, we got the police involved. They came round and set something up so that I had to press nine when he rang and they could work out where he was calling from, but they discovered it was a computer, so they couldn't track him down. We lived in a house that was all glass and I remember thinking, *Is he watching me?* That was really scary. Thankfully it's the only time I've had something like that happen, and it was before I was on TV.

How to enjoy social media
and not fall down the rabbit hole:

- *Follow accounts that make you feel really good in yourself.*

- *Be real in your posts, don't try to be someone else.*

- *If you're getting trolled, or getting lots of negative comments, step away and have a break from the platform.*

- *Remember, people only share part of their lives online. There's a whole load of other stuff going on for them behind the scenes.*

- *Try not to compare yourself to other people. Put out content that feels good for you, engage with other people's posts if you like them and don't worry about follower numbers or engagement.*

- *Remember, it's meant to be fun. Don't let it take over your life and if it's making you feel bad, reassess how much time you want to spend in a space that makes you feel worse about yourself.*

♡

'It always hurt
when people commented
on how I looked'

♡

I wish I knew ...

How stressful wedding planning is

I was so shocked when Tommy proposed. I really didn't see it coming. I hadn't clocked it at all.

He gave me the ring I asked for – yes, I basically chose it. I used to send him little messages saying, 'This is the ring I want.' It was very soon after we got engaged that we went through the really bad time and nearly split up. After that experience, when we became a stronger couple, I started going off the ring. I chose a different one a year later, and everyone was asking me what I was doing. But I felt like it was a new start, and us nearly breaking up was so associated with that first ring. Now, I feel like I'm newly engaged.

I knew Tommy would propose eventually but I didn't know when. I'm glad he didn't do it when I was pregnant; I wouldn't have wanted that. I'd have felt like he was only doing it because I *was* pregnant! But then when I had the baby I thought, *I definitely deserve a wedding proposal now, because I've just been cut open and delivered your child safely into the world.* But I still didn't imagine it would happen anytime soon.

He did it when we were away in Mexico, and it was so nice that it was caught on camera filming our show. Brody was with us too, which was so sweet.

I couldn't believe that we'd been together all those years and then when we got engaged, we started basically splitting up. Life is funny like that, but love finds a way.

Everyone says you feel different when you're married, but I wasn't sure. How can you feel different if you've been together for as long as we have? Tommy and I will have been together for over ten years when we have our big celebration in 2025! When Tommy's brother got married last year, he and his wife said it really does feel different though.

In December 2023, instead of waiting another

year for our big wedding in Spain, Tommy and I both felt it was the right moment to officially get married. On 1 December, after a challenging year – going through all the ups and downs life can throw at you, and it really did throw them at us! – we wanted to mark the end of it in a really happy and special place. We decided to enter the new year as husband and wife, in love, together. We had a small, intimate ceremony for us to enjoy as a family – and of course Brody was there, looking so cute in his suit!

We're still having a big celebration and party in Spain next year, and I'm most looking forward to everyone just being together and having a really nice time. I think we'll feel more together. More complete. And I'll hopefully have a little girl there. She'll be in her little outfit. In a dress, looking cute.

When it comes to the actual planning of the big celebration, I feel like we're getting there, but it's painstakingly slow! It probably doesn't help that I've got so much time to mull over all of the different options for everything! My wedding planner is a massive help with working out what I actually want, though. As it stands, I'm going to do a drinks reception on the Wednesday, Thursday will be a day to do what you want, Friday will be the wedding and then I want another party on the Saturday. A pool party, maybe. Because you can't expect people to travel to Spain and then only do one day of celebrations, I don't think! Tommy said he's well up for it, he wants it to be a party from the minute we start. God help me. Tommy's all or nothing. He won't drink for years and then he'll drink all day and get so drunk he can't stand up. At the wedding, he'll drink for the three days and then not drink for another year. I'll be drinking at the wedding too, but I'll probably be drunk after two glasses.

We'll have about 150 guests. Then we'll do another party in the UK for everyone who can't make it to the wedding in Spain. I get that it's expensive to travel so I want to give people the option to do a little party here instead, then they'll feel like they don't have to go away if it's too much.

The night before the actual wedding, I'll stay with my mum and sister. I would stay with the bridesmaids but there are too many. Dad will walk me down the aisle. Tommy will do a speech, but it'll be so short. He'll say, 'Hi, everyone, thanks for coming. Love you, George. Bye.' Honestly.

I'm flying to Kosovo to get a designer to make my dress. He's apparently extremely good and he'll make it from scratch. I'll have it down to the floor, with a long train, and a split up the leg. I'm not sure about a veil yet, we'll see. And definitely heels. But I'll take them off after the pictures.

I have twelve bridesmaids, with my sister included. It's really hard to pick bridesmaids because you don't always pick the people you've known forever. You could just have a really good connection with someone, a really good friendship, and want them there. When I lost the baby, I feel like everyone stepped up and was really there for me, so I wanted to include those people.

I've got my sister; and Maddie, Keri and Lauren, who are my school friends. Then I have Chloe, Sophie and Amy. They were my friends from the time I was growing up but they've carried on being friends. Then I have Beau, who does my make-up, and she's become one of my really, really good friends. Liz, my sister-in-law. And then Lydia,

Chloe and Amber from TOWIE. Amber was a TOWIE friend but she was my friend before that, too. We used to play out together when we were little.

I want everyone in the same outfits and everyone's hair will be the same: middle parting and wavy, because that suits everyone. I want them all in white, which I know some people find funny, but I think it will look really cute.

I haven't chosen the food yet because you do the food tasting in the year of the wedding. All I know is I don't want posh food, because then no one will eat it. It will be a sit-down meal because that looks better and it's easier in some ways, but the food will be stuff people know about and enjoy, not food they've never heard of. I definitely want burgers and nuggets later in the night, for when everyone's drunk.

In terms of the music, I'm looking for a band that brings a vibe all night but I'm really struggling. I've got a friend who's a wedding singer and he'll do a couple of songs, but he's also a guest at the wedding so he won't sing all night. He sings Frank Sinatra and that type of thing. I want everyone to be having the best time all night and I want to keep them up on the dance floor, so I need to find a band that will help with that.

We have to have a cake, because it's tradition, but I don't want anything too 'busy'. I want something that tastes good. I don't know if people will even eat the cake, so it needs to be something really nice or it'll be a waste. I'll keep the colours in the theme of the wedding, so the cake will be white – and then whatever colours I choose for flowers, I'll add those same colours onto the cake.

Brody will, of course, be pageboy.

Planning a wedding?

Instagram and Pinterest are the absolute best for getting ideas. I'm on there all the time. I'm really decisive because I know exactly what I want. I have a proper vision so I don't get too lost.

'Love finds a way'

I wish I knew ...
You have more power than you think

I think being the eldest of three siblings meant I took on some extra responsibility. You become the protector as the eldest, and that was quite empowering for me. I was always quite bossy as a child, too. It was always me in charge, I was the one that made the decisions. I was the first child for my mum and dad but also the first grandchild on my mum's side. When all the cousins came along, I was the leader. I was the teacher when we played schools. I was the bus driver when we pretended to go on a journey. We'd be on the stairs in my house and I'd have a little steering wheel at the bottom of the stairs, and they'd all be behind me, going up the stairs. I'd say, 'Right, off we go!' I taught them all how to dance. I think it probably gave me some confidence, being the eldest, and instructing everyone else what to do, as they did all follow me.

Saying that, I was always keen to do the right thing and it took me quite a long time to be able to say no to something I didn't want to do. I've really had to learn that. That's probably the thing that makes me feel most powerful. I know that I've got a right to say what I want. And with my show, I can say what I'm comfortable with, and what I'm not comfortable with. It's my show and it's about my life, so I can control it. I wouldn't let people tell me how to do it, or be OK with doing it any other way.

Everyone has a right to be in their power, to use their power. You are your own person and that's powerful enough. You have every right to say yes or no, depending on what you feel comfortable with. You have to learn what your power is as you get older. Now, mine is definitely the power of saying no. Back in the day, I probably would've said yes to things to make producers happy or other people happy, whereas now I do what's right for me and my family.

Remember . . .

You have the power. You get to decide how your day will pan out, what you'll have for dinner, what you'll do to relax, who you want to be friends with, how you're going to parent. You're always making decisions every single day, and knowing that is powerful. You have the power to say yes, to say no, and to reach for whatever dream you'd like to reach for.

♡

'You have to learn
what your power is
as you get older.
Mine is the power
of saying no'

♡

I wish I knew ...
That baby brain fog is real

Baby brain fog is so real. I've still got it now. It started when I was pregnant, but then when I had Brody, it was still there. It feels like my brain's never going to get back to normal.

I'm so forgetful and I don't take in information at all. I feel like I've got a bit thicker, too, like I don't know so much any more because I've been in a baby bubble for so long. Do you feel like that too?

I don't even watch the news any more. I can't tell you what's going on because downstairs it's just baby TV all day. I'm consumed by baby stuff. I have no clue about general life. I used to always have *This Morning* and *Loose Women* on. They'd be talking about what's going on in the world, but there's none of that now!

I don't try to fight the baby brain. It is what it is. It'll go one day. I might even miss it, when it's gone. I do think your brain changes when you become a mum. It expands to take in all the new information relating to your baby and life admin shuffles way down the priority list. I'll still do the essential things that have a clear deadline – like pay tax bills – but general things like calling the bank to change your address go right down to the bottom of the pile. I make my list in order of priority and if it's at the bottom, I say, 'Oh, I'll do that in a minute.' And then that minute never comes around . . .

It's quite a nice feeling being in the fog sometimes, because it feels quite safe here. For anyone who is struggling with it, just make sure you've got a good list of everything that needs to be done and start tackling the jobs, because it does feel good when you're ticking them off. Writing it down on paper automatically frees up a little bit of space in your brain. Sometimes I'll write down a task I need to do just so I can cross it off.

When I'm putting things into the diary I share with my agent, she'll reply saying, 'Are you all right, hun? You just put a meeting in for 3 a.m.?' We have a laugh. I did have two diaries – one for me and Tommy; one for work – but I kept double-booking myself, so now I've just got the main one and everything goes in there.

'I don't try to fight it'

Did you know . . .

A study by the National Library of Medicine[1] proved that 'baby brain' is an actual thing and that the radical hormonal changes that take place during pregnancy affect the brain, as well as the body.

By observing a group of first-time mothers and fathers throughout the woman's pregnancy, they were able to see the substantial changes in brain structure for the pregnant women, particularly in grey matter (a type of tissue in your brain and spinal cord that enables you to function normally day to day).

They said that the changes were highly consistent among the mothers, showing that the brain very much does respond to the pregnancy. And these changes last for at least two years post-pregnancy, perhaps longer.

---

1 Hoekzema E. et al. 'Pregnancy leads to long-lasting changes in human brain structure.' *Nature Neuroscience* 20, 287–296 (2017). https://doi.org/10.1038/nn.4458

What's amazing is that the grey matter changes during pregnancy indicate the measures of postpartum maternal attachment. So basically, baby brain is an important process for the mother-to-be as she transitions into motherhood. It helps her to form an attachment with her baby, as she hones in on their needs above all else. We might forget what we were meant to buy from the shops, but we'll remember that our baby needs feeding, for instance.

So if you're suffering with 'baby brain', know that it's meant to happen, and that it can help you to form a closer bond with your baby.

I wish I knew ...
I'd have to make hard decisions

When I go to cafés, I'll ask the waitress what she thinks I should have. My friends always take the piss out of me.

I think it's a Gemini trait because one minute I'll be saying, 'I'm doing this, and that's that.' And then I'll be out for lunch, saying, 'Do I want beans on toast or a vegetarian breakfast?' The waitress will look at me and say, 'Ooh, beans on toast.' And I'll say, 'I don't want that, I'll have a vegetarian breakfast.' But I'll have had to have a chat about it for ten minutes before deciding. I love a bit of input. It gives me the confidence to say what I really want.

We're making some big life decisions at the moment, between me and Tommy, about having more children, getting married. Obviously Tommy's also just got his ADHD diagnosis, so we're learning to live with that too. There are always going to be bumps in the road because things happen in life and you have to figure them out. There will be hurdles, but as long as I know what they might be, it's fine, I can tackle it. I can already envisage certain situations that will be tricky and we'll have to figure out how we're going to be on the same page.

With my work, I feel like I'm on a really good path at the moment. I think there will be hard decisions if something happens with the show, but while it continues to get commissioned, and I'm doing jobs I like doing – working with the right brands – I feel set.

When Brody goes to nursery, I will have three days a week to focus more on my work. At the moment, I'm a full-time mum and I'm working around Brody. It will be good when he's in nursery and I can organise myself better – and make sure all my work fits into those three days if I can. I want to enjoy my time with Brody outside of those days, making memories with him. I'm in a very lucky position where I can set those boundaries every week with my team.

'Know that it's OK to get things wrong sometimes'

When you have a big decision to make . . .

- *Take some time to mull it over, you don't have to rush into it.*

- *Speak to your people: friends, family – whoever you can trust to have your best interests at heart.*

- *Think through the pros and cons of saying yes, or saying no.*

- *Know that it's OK to get things wrong sometimes. If you go ahead and then realise you need to backtrack, that's OK.*

- *Follow your heart.*

I wish I knew ...

That friends are either forever or come and go and both are OK

I have school friends who I'm still really close to. They're from secondary school, rather than primary, but that still means I've had them for twenty years. I have my mum friends. I have my old going-out friends. And then I've got the TOWIE lot. I've got all these different groups and I introduced them, so now we're all friends.

Friends do come and go, because even though it sometimes feels like someone is a friend for life, things can change – and that's OK. Perhaps they've served a purpose for a specific time in your life when you needed them, or they needed you, and now they're not going to be a part of your life any more.

I'm sure I've served a purpose in other people's lives. It's all about timing, I think, and if you as a person at a specific point in your life need to feel loved, or comfortable, or secure. It depends on what job you're doing, or if you're single. You might have other 'single friends', and then you go and get a boyfriend and have kids, and those single friends don't always make it into the next stage of your life. When I was younger, I'd try to cling on to friendships because I liked the person, but if it's not working with the life you have now, it's OK to let them go.

It's life in a nutshell really, isn't it? You'll go through a period of having rows with your mate because they want to go out all the time and you don't. Or you get into a relationship and you don't want to be doing crazy things any more. Sometimes that winds people up, the idea that you might have changed, but that's on them.

I found it really hard when I fell out with girlfriends on TOWIE. We were just being young and stupid. But that's probably the worst time I've had, in terms of fall-outs with friends – getting into situations that didn't really need to happen. With my friends, even now, we might bicker a bit but you get over it.

I did have a good friend on TOWIE who I was eventually so upset with. There was a cheating allegation to do with Tommy on the show, and she brought it to camera. Another friend told me that she had started the rumour. She was my really good friend and that was so hurtful. I loved this friend, and I didn't understand why she'd do that to me. I confronted her on air, and she denied she said it. Tommy had denied doing anything too on air. She said that other people were talking about it and she just joined the conversation, but our producers told me that she was the one who brought it up on camera.

After that, we were never friends again. It was very easy to cut her out. At one point, she had even been accused of cheating on her boyfriend (which she also denied) and I stuck up for her, so I couldn't believe she had turned on me. She wouldn't answer my calls; I was ringing her to find out what was going on and she just wouldn't answer. She obviously wasn't a true friend, though.

I'm a very loyal friend. I always stick with you and I love having loyal people around me to protect me too.

I had one friend who was a really good friend. Or so I thought. She was in my friendship group at school. When I got my clothes shop, I feel like she got very jealous. She'd come in to see me and I'd give her so many discounts, not making any money on the clothes she was taking! In fact, it probably cost me money in the end.

I remember her saying things like, 'Oh, Daddy's bought you this shop, has he?' Really nasty stuff. She didn't know what was going on in my life. Then all of a sudden, she started promoting another shop in town. It had opened after mine and they were nicking all my ideas, contacting brands I had in and wanting to stock them too, which was weird.

When I confronted her, she basically tried saying

it was an old friend and I thought, *I've never, ever heard you mention her, I've never seen her in your life and we've been friends since we were eleven.* We fell out over that. My other friend, who was working in my shop with me, fell out with her as well because she then did the same thing to her! It was all very weird and I couldn't get over it. She tried popping up a couple times after I got on TOWIE, and I wasn't having it. If you do something like that to me, I can't be friends with you again. It's all about trust, and building you up when you're in a friendship. If they seem hell-bent on tearing you down, on not supporting you, or ever saying anything nice to you – as simple as that – then they aren't to be trusted.

My friendships with my old mates feel safe, especially my school girls. I see them for sushi and a catch-up and it doesn't matter what's going on, or how long it's been, we always have a good time. They're the ones who would bail me out of jail. I think they all got a bit annoyed when I was on TOWIE but they got used to it in the end. They liked some of the perks – like if I got a few free bottles of something at a club! It's worth remembering that your real friends might also come and go. They will come back into your life when you need them, or when it's the right time for them to re-enter your space.

I never really ventured out and made friends from the other reality TV shows. There are people I talk to who have been on *Love Island*, and the *Geordie Shore* girls are really nice. I'll always say hello and talk to them.

I feel like I still have space for new friends in my life. Becoming a mum has changed things up a bit and being out and about with Brody means I'm meeting new people. I like having a lot of people I can go out with and talk to.

They need to be loyal and trustworthy, that's what I'd want in a new friend. I can't get on with high-maintenance friends, I haven't got the time for that. Who does?! People who get annoyed if I can't see them or get the hump if I say I'll go for dinner with them but then I have to cancel because of Brody. If a friend says they can't come to my birthday for whatever reason, I don't get the hump. It's life. We're in our thirties, things happen. I would like to request from the universe some more low-maintenance friends that, when we see each other, it's like no time's passed. That's my ideal friend. Interested?

'Even though it sometimes feels like someone is a friend for life, things can change – and that's OK'

Remember . . .

- *You will have friends who come and friends who go. That's OK. Change is inevitable.*

- *If one of your friends does you over or goes behind your back, you don't need to let them stay in your life; you can wave goodbye to that friendship.*

- *That said, we all make mistakes and bicker occasionally so try to keep in check what matters and what doesn't. Forgive the stuff that doesn't really matter.*

- *Hold your good friends close. They are special and it's them who you'll turn to when the going gets tough.*

I wish I knew ...

I'm a proper extrovert

I love having people around me all the time, I'm a proper people person. But sometimes it's hard juggling seeing everyone, trying to see all my friends and keep up with everyone else's lives, because there are a lot of people in my life. I love it, because I love people – Tommy doesn't really love people – but it's quite hard to keep up when there's only seven days in the week. I'm an extrovert, Tommy's an introvert. I love people coming round to my house. It can be stressful making all the social plans but I just get on with it, I just work out how to do it. That's why I have so many lists.

When people are round – and that might be my

mates from school, some of the TOWIE girls, new friends I've made since having Brody, the nans, my sister – we just chill. Brody will be playing or watching telly and we'll drink tea and chat, to catch up on what's been going on, talk about whatever they're going through. I love supporting people and listening to their problems. But I also love hearing when good things are happening for my friends and family. I'm there for it all.

It's weird how some people feel really energised by having people around all the time, coming in and out of the house. I feel at my best when the door's open and there's a constant flow of people coming in. I know for other people, like Tommy, that is stressful instead, but then we're all different, aren't we?

Maybe it's one of the reasons I love doing the show. It means I have even more people coming round. Different people will be coming in to do my hair and make-up, or helping me choose clothes to wear to events. I make friends with everyone. My make-up woman, Beau, has become a properly good friend. She's even going to be one of my bridesmaids.

Tommy's up and down with the show, sometimes he loves it – producer of the year – other times, he says he doesn't want to do it. As I said, he doesn't love having lots of people around, unlike me. But also, he's got his work. The filming does give him a bit of a release, though, as his job is stressful. It takes him into a different space.

If I had a choice, I would never, ever be on my own. It's nice now I've got Brody, but even when it's just me and him, it doesn't always feel like there's enough energy in the room – so I'll drive round to my mum's and hang out with her and my sister. I need to be constantly surrounded. That's when I'm at my absolute happiest. But whatever type of person you are, an extrovert or an introvert, make sure you create the type of home space that makes you happy and helps you to thrive and be your best.

If you're an extrovert in a relationship with an introvert, remember: you get your energy from being around people most of the time. So if your partner feels the opposite – and gets their energy from quiet time and being alone, or being just the two of you – try to strike a balance between the two. Have date nights and nights in together watching a film, and then take yourself off out with your girlfriends for a chatty, loud, sociable night every now and again to get your extroversion fix.

♡

'It's quite hard to keep up
when there's only
seven days in the week!'

♡

I wish I knew ...
The guilt doesn't go away

♡

I feel like mum-guilt never leaves. I remember doing an away trip for a few nights and missing the first time Brody crawled. I cried. I can't remember exactly how old he was, he crawled quite late – over the age of one – but I didn't think he was going to crawl at all. And then I went away and all of a sudden, my mum and sister called and said he was crawling and I was really sad that I'd missed it. Until that moment, I hadn't felt bad about being away but missing a milestone was extremely hard.

These days, I feel guilty even if I'm just going to miss his bedtime. But then I think, *Well, I'm working and I'm doing that for him, too.* I think you never lose that guilt. I remind myself that Brody has got a great life, a really great life, because Tommy and I both work and we can provide that for him. It always pulls on my heartstrings when he says, 'Mummy, Mummy, stay,' and I've got to work. I feel the guilt but it doesn't actually stop me from doing anything. I do it and deal with the guilt. I'm doing it for me, and for him.

I feel like when you do things like that for yourself, you're then a better mum anyway. But I feel bad because he doesn't understand that yet. So often, I go without saying goodbye. The nans are good at distracting him.

It's funny, though, because when I go on a work trip, I'm always phoning home and checking in, feeling all sorts of guilt. I sometimes feel like I can conjure new feelings of guilt no one else has ever felt before. But I went on a girls' trip recently for three nights and I didn't feel bad at all because I knew I needed it. I was living my best life! It was my way of letting my hair down.

I rarely drink but on a girls' trip I do. On that

one, I was drunk the whole time! When I let myself go, I completely zone out. I did message home to check in, but it's different to when I'm on a work trip. Then, I'll be checking they got him down for his nap, asking if he's woken up. When I'm with my mates, I feel like it's not a problem; someone else will be able to deal with Brody's needs.

The smallest things make me feel guilty, though. The other day, Brody was being an absolute nightmare and I was really stressed and couldn't wait for the day to end. I was wishing for 7 p.m. to hurry up. Then as soon as he went to bed, I cried and felt so bad that I wasn't my best self with him. I wasn't as patient as I normally would be.

I don't ever feel guilty about my relationship with Tommy changing since Brody came along. I feel like that's life – we wanted a baby and that's what we did. You always wish you could spend more time together and go on more dates but the only thing I'll feel guilty about is if he asks me to go on work trips in different countries and I say no. Pre-Brody, I'd have said yes. My priority has to be Brody and he accepts that.

He recently asked me to go to America with him for two weeks; he said just bring Brody too. But it's not as easy as that. It's a long flight. The time difference would be unsettling for him. We don't even know where we'd be going out there, he'll be in business meetings all day. It's not fair on Brody. And it's not fun for us. Tommy says sometimes that he needs me to go to support him but it's not practical. Brody's starting nursery and I can't leave him to start nursery without me there. I would never leave him for two weeks anyway, so I'd be flying there for a week and then I'd have to come back on my own. So I said, 'You just have to crack on on your own this time, get your shit done. And if you need me to come back out there next time, I will.'

Tommy's OK with it. He likes that I prioritise Brody and that I'm a good mum. If he got jealous of me looking after Brody more than him, I'd be like, 'Get over it. No offence.' Or I'd just make more effort to do date nights, the two of us. He's quite cool with all that, though, we're fairly independent.

We used to do more together, but his work's more demanding now. He has to travel a lot and I'm not always going to go.

But it's not just Brody; I have my work as well and I enjoy working. We've both got our commitments. Having some space is always good too. He'll be away for two weeks and I'll miss him but I think that's healthy. We live together, we film our show together – which is full-on for the three-month period we're filming – so we do quite a lot intensely together. It's nice to have these little breaks occasionally and miss each other.

Over the years, I've felt guilt when I can't make things or do things, especially in the TOWIE days, because I was really limited in terms of what I could do outside of the show. But what can I do? It's life. If I miss birthdays because I need to be with Brody, if Tommy's away or my mum and Bev are busy, I feel guilty but then I take them for dinner another night. I make it up to them.

I used to get myself in a panic about these things, because I'm definitely an empath. I feel like as I've grown as a person, I've had to train myself not to be so empathetic. It was getting to the point where strangers would come up to me and tell me the difficult things they were going through and I'd really take it on! It's nice that they want to do that but it can be draining. I'm very spiritual, I often have readings, and they always say that people come to me with problems. I am a good mediator, as we know. But that doesn't mean it's not draining. I had to learn to listen to my body, and then release it because otherwise it would be too much. I'd be walking around with everyone's issues all day.

With my friends, if I'm saying I can't do something and they're a bit upset, I'll apologise and make another plan to make it up to them, but I'm not going to dwell on it after that. I give myself permission to move on. I just let it go. It's back to the power of saying no – I'm not going to feel bad about it if it's because I'm with Brody. So I really don't dwell. I might chat about it with Tommy and say I'm feeling a bit bad, but then we move on. You have to! You'd spend a whole lifetime dwelling on all the things that you can't, or won't, do. It's too much. Your life is your own, so own it.

Tommy, on the other hand, is not that emotional, so he doesn't really feel much guilt. I have emotional attachments, though. I cry when my mum and sister leave when they stay over. Tommy's always like, 'Why are you crying?' When we were in Spain, my mum and sister had stayed with us for a week and we dropped them at the airport. I cried all day. I was so sad. Whereas Tommy's like, 'Yes, we've got some space!' Embrace the Tommy way of thinking!

'Mum-guilt never leaves'

Dealing with mum-guilt

If you're feeling mum-guilt, it's time for some journalling . . .

One thing I'm doing really well is . . .

_____

_____

_____

One thing I'm not so proud of is . . .

_____

_____

_____

But that's OK, because . . .
[e.g. We all make mistakes]

_____

_____

_____

I wish I knew ...

Baby loss causes a sadness that never goes

In February 2023, I found out I was pregnant. I was in Spain at the time, and I must have conceived a month earlier when we were out there choosing a wedding venue. I chose the venue, and my wedding planner said, 'Right, now go and make a baby,' – and we actually did.

I was very excited. I couldn't believe the timing. At the time, it would work out that my due date was in the October and we were planning for the wedding to be the following September, so I'd have nearly a year to plan the wedding after giving birth.

We came back from Spain and told everyone. I

even shared the news on camera, for my TV show. We went for the first scan at around six weeks for reassurance, and they said everything was fine. They did say the baby was a bit small but there was a heartbeat so I wasn't worried.

I went back a couple of weeks later for another scan because I'd started bleeding. I booked a local scan in Brentwood, and they said the baby was absolutely fine. I was still bleeding but they said to me, 'Everything's fine.' I left really happy, Bev was round and my mum too. They said this can happen sometimes. We filmed the whole thing.

But I still wasn't feeling right. I had a gut feeling that something wasn't right. I said to Tommy that I needed to have another scan, and Tommy reassured me that they had said everything's fine. Normally it's the other way round but I just had this feeling. I was still bleeding and it was fresh blood now.

I called my NHS doctor for a phone consultation as I couldn't wait for an appointment but, in hindsight, hearing the blunt news over the phone that my baby wouldn't survive was hard-hitting. I wanted to seek out a second opinion so I went back to my original woman in Brentwood, told her about my symptoms, sat down with her and she said, 'I'm going to prepare you now not to see a heartbeat when we do the scan.'

I lay on the bed and suddenly we saw a heartbeat. She was shocked and so was I. But she said she was concerned about the sac around the baby; she said it looked a bit small and that could be why I was bleeding. She said either you're deficient in something or there's a chromosome problem.

Hoping it was the first option, she gave me folic acid, a strong dose of vitamin D, aspirin and a pessary that I had to do twice a day, which was not nice at all. She said, 'Go home, do all of this for a week and come back to me.' I went out and burst into tears. That week, I was full of dread. I went to church, I was praying and blessing myself with holy water.

A week later, I went back. She said, 'It's grown a bit.' We were amazed. She said: 'Come back in another week.' But a week later, she wasn't happy with the growth and said, 'Carry on taking everything and come back in two weeks.'

I went back. She said, 'The baby has still got a heartbeat but I think there's a chromosome issue.' I said, 'Are you sure?' She said, 'I think so.' She said come back in a few weeks. But we went to get a third opinion.

We googled specialists and found one of the UK's top specialists, who we were so fortunate to be able to afford. I was around ten weeks pregnant and he said, 'From what I can see, the sac is looking small but the baby has got a heartbeat, so I'm not concerned at this stage. I'm not going to tell you there's something wrong with this baby until you're twelve weeks, which is when we'll know whether the sac is actually too small.'

I went back at just over twelve weeks, and lay on the bed. I had a man doing an internal scan and another doctor in the room. He did the scan and went completely silent – it was a deafening silence. I just knew by their non-verbal communication that it wasn't right. He started saying numbers to the other guy. But I could see the baby really moving on the screen, and I could see its heartbeat. The sac did look small, though. I thought maybe it's because the baby had grown. He didn't say much, he just measured the head and the body.

He said, 'I'm going to stop now. Empty your bladder and come back.' I knew he was going to tell Tommy something. I got dressed behind a little curtain and I glimpsed Tommy's face. He gave me a look like *this is not good*. I went to the toilet, came back, put my shoes on – the room was still silent – and the doctor said, 'I'm really sorry but this baby has got a chromosome problem. We think the baby has got sixty-nine chromosomes, twenty-three more than what you should have.' He said it's a really rare condition called triploidy and it means two sperm might have hit the same egg.

I said, 'What does this mean for the baby?' He said, 'There's no survival rate.' I said, 'But the baby's moving, it's got a heartbeat.' He said, 'Chances are, you could go full term, you could have a stillborn, or you could miscarry. Or the baby could survive a couple of hours.'

I'm hysterical at this point.

He said, 'I wouldn't say this to you if I didn't mean it – even if there was a 10 per cent chance, I'd tell you. But for your own mental health, we need to get this baby out of you now.'

Obviously I'm hysterical, screaming. I kept saying, 'Are you sure, are you sure?' I'm looking at this baby moving and they're telling me it's dying but I can't see it. I wish that the baby had had no heartbeat because that would mean it was done. It sounds terrible but it feels like that would have made it less confusing.

They were saying I needed to terminate this pregnancy and it went against everything I believe in. I was screaming, uncontrollable. I took a moment, the staff were so lovely. I was saying, 'Are you sure?' The doctor looked me in the eye, held my hand and said, 'I'd never suggest terminating this pregnancy if there was a chance of it surviving. I know how much you want this baby. You've had a really traumatic time, it's been so up and down – one minute you've been happy, the next you're panicked. For you, we need to get this baby out now.'

I was in the office. They were looking at operation dates and they said, 'Right, Monday morning.' This was the Friday and they said come on Monday morning. So I left there pregnant but knowing that soon, I wasn't going to be. I just sobbed.

I got a call from the hospital, from the lady who was going to do the procedure. She said she'd moved things around so she could get me in the following morning. I put down the phone, told everyone – Tommy, my mum, Bev – and they all said this is the best thing, you can't have this hanging over you all weekend. I agreed but I was really sad, as it was my last weekend of being pregnant. I already had a bump.

I was laying there, sobbing to my mum, saying, 'I know this is the best thing and I shouldn't drag it out, but it makes me so sad this is my last night being pregnant.' I got up in the morning, went straight to the hospital – I couldn't eat – and had the procedure done.

What was so hard was that I felt like I knew the baby, as I'd seen it so much in all those scans. I was watching it grow week by week.

Also, the up and down of the situation was absolutely cruel. One week, I'd have hope; then the next week, I wouldn't. It was such a headfuck. I kept thinking, *What if this is a miracle baby?* It was seeing that heartbeat.

I lay there after the procedure – you have to be put under – and I was a bit sore but mostly, I thought, *I don't understand what's happened.* I felt empty. I still had a bump but no baby inside. The drive home was traumatic, and I was exhausted mentally and physically. I just wanted to go to sleep and not talk to anyone. It was really, really hard.

I was in bed for a few days and my mum was at mine, but a week later I started filming again. We told everyone what had happened. The film crew had been with me the whole time, documenting it. They were at the scans. They filmed me telling my parents. They were filming every moment.

I didn't know if I could do the filming, but Tommy and I had always said we'd film the good and the bad so we decided to go ahead. Also, we'd started filming it, so we needed to carry on. It was so raw at one point that I thought I couldn't talk about it, but in the end it was like therapy. When I look back, I'm glad we did film it. Especially now that I know I've helped loads of other women.

I still feel deep sadness now. When it happened, I was in shock and I felt so sad, but I didn't understand what was happening. It didn't feel real. Now, I'm just sad. I don't think that sadness will ever go. People say it doesn't go, you just learn to live with it. That's what will happen. But there's still a part of me that hasn't come back, I'm not 100 per cent myself. I'm blessed to have Brody but I feel like I'm not fully in the room any more. I don't know if it will get better when I'm pregnant again but right now I'm living month to month and I'm not pregnant.

Grief is hard. The problem with baby loss is there are triggers everywhere. I can't get away from it. Instagram is full of babies. Loads of my friends are pregnant; my sister-in-law is pregnant. People constantly ask if I'm going to have another baby. They say: *Oh, Georgia's pregnant* – because I haven't lost the weight.

I've started going to the gym, which has definitely helped me recently. I thought I might have good news this month, have a new blessing, but it hasn't happened so that hurts more. When I came on my period, it hit hard. But I'm trying to keep busy with filming. As I write this, it's actually Baby Loss Awareness week. I think I'd like to partner with a baby loss charity, to talk about our experience and help me process it and keep the memory alive.

'I still feel deep sadness now'

My advice to others going through this:

- *Don't be afraid to tell people you're pregnant before the twelve-week scan, because I needed the support when I lost my baby.*

- *Don't feel bad for getting triggered. If you're struggling with friends or family becoming pregnant, you can be happy for them but also feel bad for yourself. I found the first pregnancy I heard about especially hard to hear. I still feel sad hearing about pregnancies now. It's normal.*

- *Don't be hard on yourself. Grief never leaves you. Someone told me that the cells of your baby never leave you, so a part of your baby will always be in you.*

- *Talk about it as much as you want. When I get pregnant again, it will be my third pregnancy. And I don't want to forget my second baby. I got a tattoo of wings on my wrist and I'm going to plant a rosebush in my garden in memory.*

I wish I knew ...

How much I would want to grow my family

At the moment, my main focus is on having a baby. It feels like I can't get on with my normal life until that happens. I can't let my life flow, there's a block. I want to plan my hen do and Spain celebration but then I think, *What if I'm pregnant?* And that leads to, *When am I going to be pregnant? When am I going to have another baby?*

I don't want to put too much pressure on myself because that doesn't help. So now I'm in a situation where life goes on, so I'm getting on with it, but I'm not really, not 100 per cent, because I just desperately want to have another baby.

Tommy does too but also says I should stop putting so much pressure on it, on us, on me. He knows when I'm stressing out, and he knows it doesn't help. I know that too, but it's very frustrating when you're waiting for your body to catch up with your mind.

My body was in sync before with what I wanted, and it's really hard to experience when your body changes with all the hormones, but not with the outcome we wanted. Every month, I feel sad, because another month has passed without a baby to grow. Every month when I'm not pregnant it's mentally hard. People continue to say annoying things, like, 'Are you going to stop trying?'

I want to have a baby by our celebration in Spain. If it took that long to get pregnant, I'd be going to the doctors. It's so hard just waiting for your body to give you what you want. It's my biggest dream, right now, to have another baby. I really hope it happens.

Seeing everyone around you having babies is hard. I'm struggling with the constant triggers and I also feel bad because I want to be happy for everyone else. I know this doesn't make me a bad person. Just a normal human being.

Losing a baby never goes away. It's hard to see everyone's life moving on when a part of yours is missing.

'It's my biggest dream, right now. I really hope it happens'

It's OK to:

- *Feel sad.*

- *Have good days and bad days.*

- *Cry and get it out if need be.*

It helps to remember the baby you lost. I have a tattoo and a plaque in my bedroom.

I wish I knew ...

What the mental load was

At this moment in time, I have a lot on. I'm back doing my work, writing this book, recording my podcast, having meetings about shows, filming my own show. I'm working on a super exciting collection, and also thinking about the next series of the show. Then I've got the wedding load. The baby load. And all I can think about all day is having another baby. I've got the day-to-day life of being a mum and a partner. Plus, general life. It's quite a lot, when you write it down and look at it like that. Have you ever written your load down like that?

When you're a mum, you take on so much. Tommy's definitely got a big mental load at the moment, but the things he's thinking about and planning and doing are all kind of in the same genre. It's all work-related. I feel like mine is made up entirely of random things, connected only through me. In our home, I'm fully Brody's mum all day. Tommy might play with him for a few hours or take him out for a bit but, generally, day-to-day, it's me. I do Brody's breakfast, lunch, dinner, bath, bed. I literally *do* Brody. I of course have the nans. They're a huge support because Tommy works so much and we don't ever know what his work schedule will look like, so I wouldn't be able to rely on him. My general mental load is all Brody, with all of my different work projects fitting around him.

I felt resentful at the beginning, when I first had Brody. I felt resentful about the fact that Tommy could literally get up and go to the gym or get his hair cut or just walk out the door and know I'd be there to look after Brody. There really is such a difference between being a mum and being a dad. In a relationship like ours, a dad's life doesn't really change like a mum's does.

Tommy still has freedom, he can still do things, whereas I have to ask. I have to say to him, 'I need you to have Brody.' Whereas he doesn't say to me, 'I need you to have Brody because I'm getting my hair cut.' He just goes to get his hair cut. But if I need my hair done, or go to an event, I'll have to say, 'Right, are you around on Saturday because I need to go and do this?' I'm always around. I'm always here. It's assumed I'm always here. I get why people become full-time mums, and I also understand the mums who want to go back to work.

People say I'm lucky, working from home. And I am, I'm very blessed and lucky. I am so grateful that I've been with Brody for two and a bit years, but at the same time trying to juggle my day is hard. There are no boundaries. There are no lines. It's all blurred into one. If I work from the house, I get interrupted all day. When I'm doing day-to-day admin, Brody's there. It's a very different feeling in your brain when you are in work or admin mode, and you know your child is close.

If I can hear him, then I go into mum mode. If he sees me, he's fine. As long as he knows I'm nearby, he can go back to whoever's looking after him. But that's why I do think that it's easier to go to work than to work in the home. I say that to Tommy, when we're having debates. Tommy just gets to leave. His job's harder than mine, but he is outside the house all day. If I'm working, I'm at home. I'm doing five jobs at a time. I'm doing everything at once and my brain's exhausted. But when he leaves to go to work, he's just focusing on that job, isn't he?

I don't know if it's because I've had a break from certain areas of my career, but it feels like my brain's been asleep, like it's still on standby even when I've opened the laptop up, ready to get going. There's so much to do that it all starts swirling around in my head.

I always get insomnia when I'm feeling stressed. Now I'll write down everything that's on my mind so that I know I'm going to deal with it tomorrow. I remember one time when I was pregnant with Brody, I woke up thinking we had to pay the electric bill. It was in Tommy's name and I remember it popped in my head that it was a day late. It caused me so much distress, I stayed up for three hours panicking and by the time it was 5 a.m., I tried calling the company, thinking it would be open. I was making scenarios up in my head, thinking that he was going to get a bad credit rating because of this £180 bill and then we wouldn't ever be able to get a mortgage. I caused myself to enter the most mental state ever.

I remember calling Tommy's dad at 7 a.m. being like, 'Mark, do you think Tommy will get bad credit?' He was like, 'No, it's going to be OK.' It was all very dramatic. But that's the kind of shit I do. I'm laidback in social situations but then I get worried about things like that. Are you the same? When I'm feeling it's all too much, I have a little cry on my own because I feel like you've got to get it out. Or I'll vent to my mum or Tommy. But do you know, a list definitely helps, because then I can prioritise what I need to be doing right now. It's back to taking one day at a time.

♡

'When you're a mum,
you take on so much'

♡

Did you know . . .

According to the Office for National Statistics (ONS), three in four mothers with dependent children (75.6 per cent) are in work in the UK, the highest level for the past twenty years. And yet we are still doing significantly more unpaid childcare – 84 minutes a day, while the men do an average of 55 minutes a day. On top of that, we do an average of 169 minutes of housework each day, while men do just 106 minutes.[2]

So we're balancing paid work with a whole lot more childcare and doing more housework. And we haven't even touched on the 'mental load' side of it (planning social events for the family, organising

---

2 Murphy, R. et al. 'Families and the labour market, UK: 2021', Office for National Statistics (2022). Available at: https://www.ons.gov.uk/employmentandlabourmarket/peopleinwork/employmentandemployeetypes/articles/familiesandthelabourmarketengland/2021 [Accessed 13 September 2023]

play dates, finding nursery and school places, remembering to pay nursery fees, buying uniforms and so on).

A study from the Australian Institute of Family Studies found that for '78 per cent of households, the mental load was "always or usually" carried by the mother. In one third, it was "always" the mother.'[3] That's a lot of extra thinking load on the mother, isn't it? Perhaps that's why I'm so obsessed with writing lists. On that note . . .

3 Tuohy, Wendy. 'When it comes to kids, mothers are saddled with the "mental load"', *Sydney Morning Herald* (June 16 2022). Available at: https://www.smh.com.au/national/when-it-comes-to-kids-mothers-are-saddled-with-the-mental-load-20220616-p5au46.html [accessed 13 September 2023]

I wish I knew ...

How important lists would be

- Lists get the mental load out of your brain.
- They clear space in your head.
- You have the satisfaction of ticking things off.
- I have day lists and weekly lists.
- I write a list when I'm ordering Chinese on a Saturday night.
- I make a list before a holiday and weekends away.
- When someone looks after Brody, I create a very long list, so it's more like a book, really ...
- I wrote lists as a child, too, about what presents I wanted for my birthday, for example!

- Lists have to be written using pen and paper, not on your phone.

- Writing lists is a de-stress mechanism. It's now out of your head, and you're not going to forget it.

- Lists make me feel more relaxed, less anxious.

- I have a little book to write all my lists in.

- It doesn't matter if you forget things on the list – just get it all down and you'll feel better.

- Now I'm a mum, lists are one of the most important ways I can remember everything.

- Having random lists dotted around the house isn't useful, it's stressful! Write them all together or store them in one place so you know where to go when you're feeling overwhelmed.

- If there are too many things on your list and nothing on your partner's, they need to re-evaluate the list load!

- Lists then become useful evidence of all of the amazing things you have managed to organise, keep track of and tick off.

- So keep making lists, keep ticking things off.

♡

'Just get it all down
and you'll feel better'

♡

I wish I knew ...

How the online community you build will be there for you, no matter what

I love my Instagram community. I started my account in 2014 and have built up a space which is so positive and lovely. My followers feel like my friends, they're all loyal – to me and each other – and are just like my mates. They give me advice whenever I need it, and we have the best conversations together, replying to each other and having chats. It's the best experience, to know there are so many people online who are behind you, who are there for each other.

If I ever post and say, 'I'm going on holiday,

I need tips…' they're there, with the best recommendations. If I'm ever feeling down, people let me know it's not just me.

My community have been there for me throughout everything. Losing my baby in 2023, and Tommy's ADHD journey. Anything I've been through, they've been there for me.

The Instagram community has helped me to grow because, through them, I have learnt so much. We share advice, worries, anxieties, small wins in life. I give advice to them too, in my agony aunt role I can't seem to escape from! We all reassure each other that we're OK, that we're doing the right thing for ourselves. Although they definitely tell you if you're doing the wrong thing, too! But it's nice to know they have my back, and I have theirs.

At this point, there's not much I wouldn't show on social media. I wouldn't share family things if they weren't mine to share. Or if Tommy tells me something in private, of course I'm not going to be announcing that on Instagram. But I'll share pretty much everything else! My most honest posts always get the most engagement because that is me being real, opening up. If I woke up tomorrow and Instagram had vanished, I'd be incredibly sad to feel so disconnected. I'd feel like I didn't know who to talk to suddenly. I love talking to people on Instagram, as well as my real-life friends. The online world doesn't replace the real world, but there's space for both.

I hope that what my followers see is that I'm just a normal girl, doing my best, talking honestly about life and motherhood, and what makes me feel better about myself. That's what I want to share, and who I continually want to be.

Building a great community on Instagram

Here are my tips:

- *Be your authentic self.*

- *Share the real you – people know when you're not being yourself.*

- *Be open and honest – people don't want to see the filtered, unrealistic version, they want the real, gritty you.*

- *Put time into it. Post daily, if you can (I'm not always so good at that but I was at the start).*

- *Interact with people: ask questions, answer questions.*

- *You do you.*

♡

'They have my back,
and I have theirs'

♡

Your

Journal

Thank you so much for reading my book. I hope parts of it have connected with your life and experiences, and that it's left you feeling a little less alone. To end, I wanted to share some coaching exercises with you in case you want to go on to think about your own life – what's working; what you'd like to change – and make some plans. Here are some journal prompts for you to work through. Let me know how you get on by sharing on Instagram and tagging me @georgiakousoulou. I'd really love to hear from you.

♡ 1 ♡

How are you feeling right now?

○
○ _____
○
○ _____
○
○ _____
○
○ _____
○
○ _____
○
○ _____
○
○ _____
○
○ _____
○
○ _____
○
○ _____
○
○ _____
○

♡ 2 ♡

What's one thing you're really
proud of yourself for right now?

♡ **3** ♡

Write down three things you love about yourself . . .

♡ 4 ♡

Name five things you're feeling grateful for:

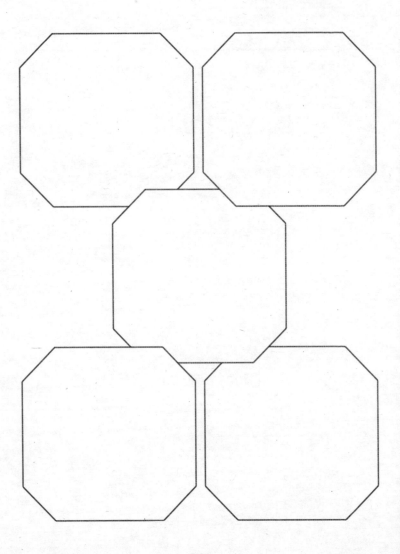

♡ **5** ♡

What would you like to manifest in your life?

♡ 6 ♡

What does your dream life look like?

7

What's missing from your life?

♡ **8** ♡

Who can you share your dreams with?

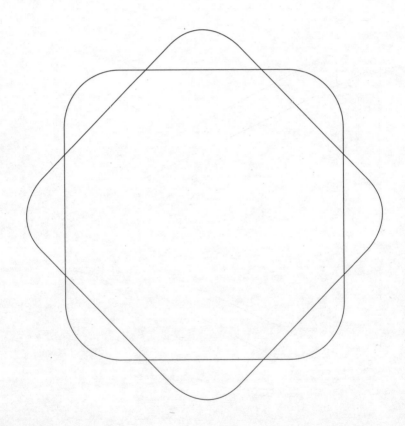

♡ *9* ♡

What one step can you take today
towards your dream life?

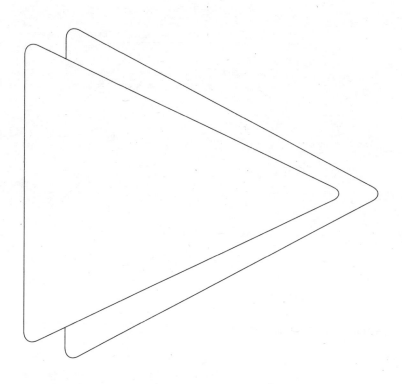

♡ 10 ♡

How will it feel, once you've
manifested all of the above?